THE PELICAN SHAKESPEARE

GENERAL EDITOR : ALFRED HARBAGE

AB5

HAMLET

WILLIAM SHAKESPEARE

The Tragedy of
Hamlet
Prince of Denmark

EDITED BY WILLARD FARNHAM

PENGUIN BOOKS

BALTIMORE · MARYLAND

This edition first published 1957
Reprinted 1959, 1960, 1961, 1963 (twice), 1965, 1966, 1967
Penguin Books Inc.
3300 Clipper Mill Road, Baltimore, Maryland 21211

Printed in the United States of America

CONTENTS

SHAKESPEARE AND HIS STAGE

William Shakespeare was christened in Holy Trinity Church, Stratford-on-Avon, April 26, 1564. His birth is traditionally assigned to April 23rd. He was the eldest of four boys and two girls who survived infancy in the family of John Shakespeare, glover and trader of Henley Street, and his wife Mary Arden, daughter of a small landowner of Wilmcote. In 1568 John was elected Bailiff (equivalent to Mayor) of Stratford, having already filled the minor municipal offices. The town maintained for the sons of the burgesses a free school, taught by a university graduate and offering preparation in Latin sufficient for university entrance; its early registers are lost, but there can be little doubt that Shakespeare received the formal part of his education in this school.

On November 27, 1582, a license was issued for the marriage of William Shakespeare (aged eighteen) and Ann Hathaway (aged twenty-six), and on May 26, 1583, their child Susanna was christened in Holy Trinity Church. The inference that the marriage was forced upon the youth is natural but not inevitable; betrothal was legally binding at the time, and was sometimes regarded as conferring conjugal rights. Two additional children of the marriage, the twins Hamnet and Judith, were christened on February 2, 1585. Meanwhile the prosperity of the elder Shakespeares had declined, and William was impelled to seek a career outside Stratford.

The tradition that he spent some time as a country teacher is old but unverifiable. Because of the absence of records his early twenties are called the "lost years," and only one thing about them is certain – that at least some of these years were spent in winning a place in the acting profession. He may have begun as a provincial trouper, but by 1592 he was established in London and prominent enough to be attacked. In a pamphlet of that year, *Groatsworth of Wit*, the ailing Robert Greene complained of the neglect which university writers like himself had suffered from actors, one of whom was daring to set up as a playwright:

> ... an upstart crow beautified with our feathers, that with his *Tiger's heart wrapt in a player's hide* supposes he is as well able to bombast out a blank verse as the best of you, and being an absolute Johannes-factotum, is in his own conceit the only Shake-scene in a country.

The pun on his name, and the parody of his line "O tiger's heart wrapt in a woman's hide" (*III Henry VI*), pointed clearly to Shakespeare. Some of his admirers protested, and Henry Chettle, the editor of Greene's pamphlet, saw fit to apologize:

> I am as sorry as if the original fault had been my fault, because myself have seen his demeanor no less civil than he excellent in the quality he professes. Besides divers of worship have reported his uprightness of dealing, which argues his honesty, and his facetious grace in writing that approves his art. (Prefatory epistle, *Kind Heart's Dream*)

The plague closed the London theatres for many months in 1593–94, denying the actors their livelihood. To this period belong Shakespeare's two narrative poems, *Venus and Adonis* and *Rape of Lucrece*, both dedicated to the Earl

8

of Southampton. No doubt the poet was rewarded with a gift of money as usual in such cases, but he did no further dedicating and we have no reliable information on whether Southampton, or anyone else, became his regular patron. His sonnets, first mentioned in 1598 and published without his consent in 1609, are intimate without being explicitly autobiographical. They seem to commemorate the poet's friendship with an idealized youth, rivalry with a more favored poet, and love affair with a dark mistress; and his bitterness when the mistress betrays him in conjunction with the friend; but it is difficult to decide precisely what the "story" is, impossible to decide whether it is fictional or true. The real distinction of the sonnets, at least of those not purely conventional, rests in the universality of the thoughts and moods they express, and in their poignancy and beauty.

In 1594 was formed the theatrical company known until 1603 as the Lord Chamberlain's Men, thereafter as the King's Men. Its original membership included, besides Shakespeare, the beloved clown Will Kempe and the famous actor Richard Burbage. The company acted in various London theatres and even toured the provinces, but it is chiefly associated in our minds with the Globe Theatre built on the south bank of the Thames in 1599. Shakespeare was an actor and joint owner of this company (and its Globe) through the remainder of his creative years. His plays, written at the average rate of two a year, together with Burbage's acting won it its place of leadership among the London companies.

Individual plays began to appear in print, in editions both honest and piratical, and the publishers became increasingly aware of the value of Shakespeare's name on the title pages. As early as 1598 he was hailed as the leading English dramatist in the *Palladis Tamia* of Francis Meres:

9

As Plautus and Seneca are accounted the best for Comedy and Tragedy among the Latins, so Shakespeare among the English is the most excellent in both kinds for the stage: for Comedy, witness his *Gentlemen of Verona*, his *Errors*, his *Love labors lost*, his *Love labors won* [*Taming of the Shrew?*], his *Midsummers night dream*, & his *Merchant of Venice;* for Tragedy, his *Richard the 2*, *Richard the 3*, *Henry the 4*, *King John*, *Titus Andronicus*, and his *Romeo and Juliet*.

The note is valuable, both in indicating Shakespeare's prestige and in helping us to establish a chronology. In the second half of his writing career, history plays gave place to the great tragedies; and farces and light comedies gave place to the problem plays and symbolic romances. In 1623, seven years after his death, his former fellow actors, John Hemming and Henry Condell, cooperated with a group of London printers in bringing out his plays in collected form. The volume is generally known as the First Folio.

Shakespeare had never severed his relations with Stratford. His wife and children may sometimes have shared his London lodgings, but their home was Stratford. His son Hamnet was buried there in 1596, and his daughters Susanna and Judith were married there in 1607 and 1616 respectively. (His father, for whom he had secured a coat of arms and thus the privilege of writing himself gentleman, died in 1601, his mother in 1608.) His considerable earnings in London, as actor-sharer, part owner of the Globe, and playwright, were invested chiefly in Stratford property. In 1597 he purchased for £60 New Place, one of the two most imposing residences in the town. A number of other business transactions, as well as minor episodes in his career, have left documentary records. By 1611 he was in a position to retire, and he seems gradually to have withdrawn from theatrical activity in order to live in Stratford. In March, 1616, he made a will, leaving token bequests to Burbage, Hemming, and Condell, but the bulk of his estate to his family. The most famous feature of the will, the bequest of the second-best bed to his wife, reveals nothing about Shakespeare's marriage; the quaintness of the provision seems commonplace to those familiar with ancient testaments. Shakespeare died April 23, 1616, and was buried in the Stratford church where he had been christened. Within seven years a monument was erected to his memory on the north wall of the chancel. Its portrait bust and the Droeshout engraving on the title page of the First Folio provide the only likenesses with an established claim to authenticity. The best verbal vignette was written by his rival Ben Jonson, the more impressive for being imbedded in a context mainly critical:

> ... I loved the man, and do honor his memory (on this side idolatry) as much as any. He was indeed honest, and of an open and free nature: he had an excellent fancy, brave notions, and gentle expressions. ... (*Timber or Discoveries*, c. 1623–30)

The reader of Shakespeare's plays is aided by a general knowledge of the way in which they were staged. The King's Men acquired a roofed and artificially lighted theatre only toward the close of Shakespeare's career, and then only for winter use. Nearly all his plays were designed for performance in such structures as the Globe – a three-tiered amphitheatre with a large rectangular platform extending to the center of its yard. The plays were staged by daylight, by large casts brilliantly costumed, but with only a minimum of properties, without scenery, and quite possibly without intermissions. There was a rear stage balcony for action "above," and a curtained rear recess for "discoveries" and other special effects, but by far the major portion of any play was enacted upon the projecting platform, with episode following episode in swift succession, and with shifts of time and place signaled the audience only by the momentary clearing of the stage between the episodes. Information about the identity of the characters and, when necessary, about the time and place of the action was incorporated in the dialogue. No additional indications of place have been inserted in the present editions; these are apt to obscure the original fluidity of structure, with the emphasis upon action and speech rather than scenic background. The acting, including that of the youthful apprentices to the profession who performed the parts of women, was highly skillful, with a premium placed upon grace of gesture and beauty of diction. The audiences, a cross section of the general public, commonly numbered a thousand, sometimes more than two thousand. Judged by the type of plays they applauded, these audiences were not only large but also perceptive.

THE TEXTS OF THE PLAYS

About half of Shakespeare's plays appeared in print for the first time in the folio volume of 1623. The others had been published individually, usually in quarto volumes, during his lifetime or in the six years following his death. The copy used by the printers of the quartos varied greatly in merit, sometimes representing Shakespeare's true text.

sometimes only a debased version of that text. The copy used by the printers of the folio also varied in merit, but was chosen with care. Since it consisted of the best available manuscripts, or the more acceptable quartos (although frequently in editions other than the first), or of quartos corrected by reference to manuscripts, we have good or reasonably good texts of most of the thirty-seven plays.

In the present series, the plays have been newly edited from quarto or folio texts depending, when a choice offered, upon which is now regarded by bibliographical specialists as the more authoritative. The ideal has been to reproduce the chosen texts with as few alterations as possible, beyond occasional relineation, expansion of abbreviations, and modernization of punctuation and spelling. Emendation is held to a minimum, and such material as has been added, in the way of stage directions and lines supplied by an alternative text, has been enclosed in square brackets.

None of the plays printed in Shakespeare's lifetime were divided into acts and scenes, and the inference is that the author's own manuscripts were not so divided. In the folio collection, some of the plays remained undivided, some were divided into acts, and some were divided into acts and scenes. During the eighteenth century all of the plays were divided into acts and scenes, and in the Cambridge edition of the mid-nineteenth century, from which the influential Globe text derived, this division was more or less regularized and the lines were numbered. Many useful works of reference employ the act-scene-line apparatus established by the Globe text.

Since the act-scene division thus established is obviously convenient, but is of very dubious authority so far as Shakespeare's own structural principles are concerned, or the original manner of staging his plays, a problem is presented to modern editors. In the present series the act-scene division of the Globe text is retained marginally, and may be viewed as a reference aid like the line numbering. A printer's ornament marks the points of division when these points have been determined by a cleared stage indicating a shift of time and place in the action of the play, or when no harm results from the editorial assumption that there is such a shift. However, at those points where the established division is clearly misleading — that is, where continuous action has been split up into separate "scenes" — the ornament is omitted and the distortion corrected. This mechanical expedient seemed the best means of combining utility and accuracy.

The General Editor.

INTRODUCTION

Vicissitudes of literary taste and temper in the present age have not weakened the hold of *Hamlet* upon viewer and reader, however much they have changed it. Probably they have made it stronger than ever before, stronger even than it was for the last age of men, in the nineteenth century. This is saying much, for men in the nineteenth century helped mightily to make *Hamlet* the most acted and most written-about of Shakespeare's plays. They earnestly accepted its challenge to understanding.

That from which this challenge issues, stamped with a name in words given by Shakespeare to Hamlet himself— "you would pluck out the heart of my mystery" (III, ii, 351-52) – has come to be called the Hamlet mystery by many. Here and there it has been called so with resignation, sometimes hopelessly, but even in its guise of insolubility it can still command critical statement about its being.

It is already plain that the twentieth century will add perception that will matter to the Hamlet tradition in our culture. What it adds will be, like such an addition by any other age, a characteristic enlargement of Shakespeare's dramatic achievement. After a lapse of centuries an extension of perception for a constantly lived-with and experienced work of art like *Hamlet* is an extension of the original creation much to be reckoned with for its revelation of a complex vitality. The new creation comes about not only because the author has conceived form capable of long-continuing growth but also because a late age of posterity, despite the variety of contributions made by former ages, has conceived form into which growth can proceed.

What we in this age seem bent on giving to *Hamlet* is greatly enlarged scope. We are sure enough of ourselves to think of this as meaning a new breadth, and we may hope that it will mean also a new depth. For a long time after Shakespeare there was no generally recognized Hamlet mystery; Hamlet seems to have been for most men a courageous prince who found it understandably hard to take revenge on a shrewd and powerful king. By the nineteenth century the mystery was well established. It was troublesome enough but it could usually be kept within close bounds – that is, within the outlines of Hamlet the man realistically considered as someone who in all essential qualities, however exceptional they might be, could be judged by common sense as a walking and talking inhabitant of the critic's own age. A further limitation came from much thinking that the key to Hamlet's tragedy was probably some one dominant thing such as unstable nervous quality, or shock from his father's death and his mother's hasty remarriage, or melancholy pessimism, or sensitivity unfitting him for the crass burden of his duty to take revenge, or delight in thought unfitting him for crucial action. Such ideas were all, of course, well worth the having, and they shook down into a corpus that will be a lasting part of the Hamlet tradition. But they did not offer enough satisfaction to keep critics from hastening on to other searchings.

Our twentieth-century searchings have become less and less confined, even when they have been within the personal creation that is Hamlet. Hamlet psychology, still very much alive in an age that has produced Freud and Jung, is now not content with merely a homely reading of Hamlet's character by everyday use of heart and mind. The field of Elizabethan psychology has been carefully explored for principles applicable to Hamlet, and thus there has been a fitting of his creation into the history of ideas. With the application of modern psychological theories – especially and most inevitably those having to do with the ancient family triad of father, mother, and child – there has been an expansion of his persona to take account of a dark abysm of the human self from which can come to anyone, as is thought, tensely opposed feelings for both father and mother, and from which, we are to understand, there comes to Hamlet so much emotional conflict with regard to his uncle the King as a substitute father image, married to his mother, that his hate cannot achieve the murder of the King before his bringing, by hesitation, of death to both his mother and himself. Hamlet, indeed, may seem to have been shaped to order for psychoanalysis. In modern psychology an extension of the Hamlet creation, truly meaningful whether one responds to it or not, has been made by the coming together with a startling show of affinity of something in us and something in Shakespeare.

Elizabethan, nineteenth-century, and twentieth-century psychologies often invite us to see within Hamlet some severe seizure of the soul which is close to disease, if not actually disease, and is the more easily thought of in these terms because of the dominant disease imagery running through the play. A Hamlet viewed as thus stricken can be found to have the tragic flaw in an extreme form. Frequently enough an idea has been held that Hamlet shows an exceptionally noble nature and that in this there is, and should be, a classic flaw to make his drama a tragedy. Sometimes the flaw has seemed by no means to be disease-like or wholly undesirable but to take a paradoxical coloring of good from the nobility in which it appears. Yet it has been conceived to be no less an explanatory flaw for all that and necessarily to be delimited, even in the face of mounting disagreement as to what it is exactly.

A part of the present releasing of the Hamlet mystery from its former bounds takes Hamlet the created personality into a realm of criticism where the time-honored idea of the tragic flaw suddenly loses validity. Here there is the thought that imperfection in the hero cannot yield even a part of the meaning in his tragedy by providing some show of justice for what happens to him as an individual. But here at the same time a conception of Hamlet's having nobility of nature remains, and it may go so far as to make him into a type of human perfection. The Hamlet mystery may thus turn into something like a mystery of Hamlet's martyrdom, where whatever makes it mystery tends to be found outside the character of an individual Hamlet in the character of man in general and in the character of the universe which produces the common predicament of man. Man must act, but all action involves him in evil. It is a finding in the content of *Hamlet* that our age has perhaps been qualified to make by its rediscovery of some forgotten powers of evil in human life and by its interpretation of these in recent literature. In such an area of criticism the question is bound to rise, and does rise, whether *Hamlet* is after all a tragedy, whether it is not a drama worthy perhaps to stand with the greatest tragedies but of a kind peculiar to itself. Yet most critics still seem not of a mind to release *Hamlet* from an obligation to show tragic form.

It is remarkable that *Hamlet* should so perplex the mind and at the same time work so little confusion in the heart. It has supremely that which can make us forget our questions when we give ourselves over to it. Probably no other tragic hero of Shakespeare's equals Hamlet in drawing from the observer that most profound pity which is really as much admiration as pity, and is perfectly tragic because there is no condescension in it. It seems impossible not to forgive Hamlet his brutalities to Ophelia, Polonius, or Rosencrantz and Guildenstern, for they are washed out in our feeling if not in our thinking. He should not be made, we believe, to suffer fools gladly, he the superior spirit to add that suffering to his load.

Perhaps more strongly than anything else pity senses the terrible loneliness of Hamlet. The idealism which moves him to a life-and-death struggle with imprisoning evil is so complex, including even a composition of low comedy with high seriousness, that his single companion, the good but all too solemn Horatio, must always be alien to it. The way in which Horatio fails him in the gravediggers' scene – " 'Twere to consider too curiously" (V, i, 193) – is a part of the tragedy, and no minor one. Love desired is always falling away from Hamlet – love in father, in mother, in Ophelia. The poetry that circles about him makes us know that the Prince of Denmark goes through darkness and waste places "most dreadfully attended."

A part of the *Hamlet* that troubles the mind's eye seems to come from Shakespeare's absorption, with sympathies not at all narrow, of a story that had already had a development of meaning at different depths in different ages. This development had taken place in some rather widespread folklore, in a sophisticated literary account of "Amlethus" in the twelfth-century *Historia Danica* of Saxo Grammaticus (printed in 1514), in a very free version of Saxo's account in the fifth volume of the *Histoires Tragiques* of François de Belleforest (1576), and in an old play about Hamlet on the English stage. Concerning the pre-Shakespearean *Hamlet* we know little. A not very revelatory passage in Thomas Nashe's epistle to Robert Greene's *Menaphon* contains a reference to "whole Hamlets, I should say handfuls, of tragicall speeches" as being lifted from Seneca, which indicates that a *Hamlet* was on the stage by 1589, the date of *Menaphon*, and that it was a Senecan tragedy. Some even more tantalizing words of Nashe's in the same passage have led many to believe that Thomas Kyd, the author of the Senecan *Spanish Tragedy*, wrote this old *Hamlet*. A performance of it is recorded for 1594 and a glimpse of a part of its action comes in 1596 in Thomas Lodge's *Wits Miserie* with a description of a countenance "pale as the Visard of ye ghost which cried so miserally at ye Theator like an oister wife, *Hamlet, revenge*." Shakespeare's *Hamlet*, in the present state of our knowledge, may be dated 1600–1601. Mainly its story follows that in Belleforest. An English translation of Belleforest, *The Hystorie of Hamblet*, was published in 1608 and seems to have been affected somewhat by Shakespeare's play. It remains to mention one more Hamlet play, the unpraiseworthy German piece *Der Bestrafte Brudermord*, the origin of which is problematic, but which seems to have derived mainly from an early acting version of Shakespeare's *Hamlet*. The German play was printed as late as 1781 from a manuscript dated 1710.

Some have thought that the Hamlet mystery has been put forever beyond our understanding by the loss of the older English *Hamlet*, the so-called *Ur-Hamlet*. Some have gone so far as to make out that Shakespeare was overwhelmed by matter drawn from the *Ur-Hamlet*, which turned out to be so unmanageable as he built around it that the result was incomprehensibility for his joined whole. That way lies an accusation that *Hamlet* is a failure as a piece of dramatic art, and the accusation has been made more than once. Doubtless Shakespeare found the *Ur-Hamlet* of some avail, and doubtless the *Ur-Hamlet* was a rude play befitting the dramatic immaturity of its time, with a quality very different from the mature Shakespearean. But it would seem probable that when he wrote *Hamlet* Shakespeare was beyond being overwhelmed by an old play he wanted to use. He was almost ready to melt and recast one with complete mastery to make *King Lear*. As for *Hamlet*'s being a dramatic or literary failure, the answer of course is that our western culture has forcefully refused to have it so, and on the contrary has given it esteem of the highest. It is for western man to keep on asking why, as there seems to be no danger of his ceasing to do.

As he asks why, it is for western man to realize that he is posing questions about truth itself, about the glorious but also terrifying lack of simplicity that truth shows – and shows in special ways within his own culture – according to a Shakespearean structure of dramatic and poetic images. Here, I would say, is the Hamlet problem of Hamlet problems, one whose recognition lets us know why, after all, there must be many Hamlet problems and various answers to them, yet a gathering together of these into some containing oneness.

The theme of unsimple truth comes early into the Hamlet story. Saxo's Amlethus pretends madness to protect himself until he can get revenge upon the uncle who has killed his father and married his mother. There is no complication of soul-searching and delay in his taking of revenge. He merely bides his time. But there is complication in his procedure of saying things that will make those around him think he does not have the wit to accomplish his revenge. He has not merely that wit but the greater wit to deceive only by being truthful, by turning toward the simple swordsmen who surround him faces of the truth that they do not recognize. He has compulsion never in deepest consequence to destroy truth and he delights in following truth toward a mastery of its complexity. He mingles "craft and candor" to let no word of his "lack truth." There is in him something of primitive riddling, but that is not all. When his uncle's followers think to have sport with Amlethus on the seashore as with a simpleton and bid him look at the meal, meaning the sand, they fully expect that he will take the sand for meal. He not only takes it so; he makes it so in truth. His reply is that it has "been ground small by hoary tempests of the ocean." Here we suddenly know that we are witnessing in fully acceptable form a demonstration of the wide division between the truth of things and the truth of spirit, and the annihilation of this division in the truth of poetry. Such matter as this is largely replaced in Belleforest by a too simple moralizing but not, certainly, in Shakespeare.

In *Hamlet* the theme of unsimple truth is so abundantly restored and so subtly extended that it is everywhere in the action and the poetry. Hamlet at his first appearance begins a searching of the complexity of truth by means of word play and idea play that is carried on throughout the drama; the craft and candor of his dark rejection of sonship to the King and of royal sun-like favor from him, in the punning words "I am too much in the sun" (I, ii, 67), are right Hamlet substance and right introduction to much of the tragedy that comes later. It is by no means only in words and ideas of the moment that Hamlet stands between truths both to divide and unite them. In the large he stands thus between whole worlds of truths in our culture: between the world of an uncivilized heroic past going back even behind Christianity and that of a civilized present;

between the world of medieval faith and other-worldliness and that of modern doubt and this-worldliness. In the same way he stands between the truth of angel-like and god-like man and that of man the quintessence of dust, or, in a realm of complete abstraction, between the truth of love and that of hate. There are, needless to say, countless variations in *Hamlet* on the theme of unsimple truth.

It may be said that *Hamlet* is indeed about the pursuit of revenge but most deeply about the pursuit of truth, and that the two pursuits come together to give form to the action of the tragedy. By meeting and testing his father's ghost Hamlet gains truth that seems adequate. It proves on second thought to be not enough. By testing the King with the play within the play he gains truth "more relative than this." Here is the high point of a rising action. Now comes a testing by circumstance of truth that Hamlet has gained with his own testing. He has the chance to kill the praying King. For some reason (we ourselves never stop testing to find it) he loses at this moment of opportunity all truth he has won about revenge as a crying *immediate* need. He fails to kill the King and thus makes possible the killing of Polonius, which starts a falling action that carries him to death — and ironically to attainment of his revenge, a revenge that takes being from tragic defeat, not a revenge in simple truth such as the revenger seeks. Just before the end, to sharpen the irony, Hamlet uneasily tests his need for revenge against the King all over again, showing inability to make secure in simplicity whatever of lost truth he has regained:

> . . . is't not perfect conscience
> To quit him with this arm? And is't not to be damned

To let this canker of our nature come
In further evil?

Hamlet dies on the search for truth that all men die on.
But his tragedy has a richness of texture all its own, not only
within and around the seeker but also within and around
what is sought.

University of California　　　　　WILLARD FARNHAM

Note on the text: Hamlet is preserved in three distinct but related early
texts: first, the corrupt and abbreviated acting version in the "bad" quarto
of 1603; second, the version "newly imprinted and enlarged to almost as
much again as it was, according to the true and perfect coppie" in the
"good" quarto of 1604–05 (now usually regarded, but without complete
assurance, as printed from Shakespeare's own draft); and third, the version
in the 1623 folio (now usually regarded, but again without complete assurance, as printed from the prompt-book of Shakespeare's acting company). The present edition is based on the quarto of 1604–05 with a
minimum of emendation, but, in view of the manifest faultiness of the
quarto printing, with occasional deference to readings in the folio, and
even with an eye on the 1603 quarto. Enclosed in square brackets are all
additions to the quarto stage directions, as well as additions of whole lines
or more of dialogue from the folio. (The longer passages thus added are
II, ii, 237–66, 330–54; IV, v, 161–63; V, i, 32–35; V, ii, 68–80.) The act-
scene division supplied marginally is that of the Globe text. The texts of
the quartos are undivided, and that of the folio almost so since there is no
scene division in the first act after I, iii, 1, and no division of any kind after
II, ii, 1. It is a common complaint that the act division of the Globe text
is mechanical and inorganic, but, as explained in the general foreword, it
is supplied in the present edition only for reference purposes.

The Tragedy of Hamlet
Prince of Denmark

[Names of the Actors

Claudius, King of Denmark
Hamlet, son to the late, and nephew to the present, *King*
Polonius, Lord Chamberlain
Horatio, friend to Hamlet
Laertes, son to Polonius
Voltemand
Cornelius
Rosencrantz
Guildenstern } *courtiers*
Osric
A Gentleman
A Priest
Marcellus
Bernardo } *officers*
Francisco, a soldier
Reynaldo, servant to Polonius
Players
Two Clowns, gravediggers
Fortinbras, Prince of Norway
A Norwegian Captain
English Ambassadors
Gertrude, Queen of Denmark, mother to Hamlet
Ophelia, daughter to Polonius
Ghost of Hamlet's Father
*Lords, Ladies, Officers, Soldiers, Sailors, Messengers, Attend-
ants*

Scene
Elsinore]

THE TRAGEDY OF HAMLET
PRINCE OF DENMARK

❧

Enter Bernardo and Francisco, two sentinels.　　　　I, i

Bernardo. Who's there?

Francisco. Nay, answer me. Stand and unfold yourself.

Bernardo. Long live the king!

Francisco. Bernardo?

Bernardo. He.　　　　　　　　　　　　　　　　　　　　5

Francisco. You come most carefully upon your hour.

Bernardo. 'Tis now struck twelve. Get thee to bed, Fran-
　cisco.

Francisco. For this relief much thanks. 'Tis bitter cold,
　And I am sick at heart.

Bernardo. Have you had quiet guard?

Francisco.　　　　　　　　　　　　Not a mouse stirring.　10

Bernardo. Well, good night.
　If you do meet Horatio and Marcellus,
　The rivals of my watch, bid them make haste.

Enter Horatio and Marcellus.

Francisco. I think I hear them. Stand, ho! Who is there?

Horatio. Friends to this ground.

I, i, 13 *rivals* sharers

27

15 *Marcellus.*   And liegemen to the Dane.
   Francisco. Give you good night.
   Marcellus.   O, farewell, honest soldier.
       Who hath relieved you?
   Francisco.   Bernardo hath my place.
       Give you good night.   *Exit Francisco.*
   Marcellus.   Holla, Bernardo!
   Bernardo.   Say —
       What, is Horatio there?
   Horatio.   A piece of him.
20 *Bernardo.* Welcome, Horatio. Welcome, good Marcellus.
   Horatio. What, has this thing appeared again to-night?
   Bernardo. I have seen nothing.
   Marcellus. Horatio says 'tis but our fantasy,
       And will not let belief take hold of him
25   Touching this dreaded sight twice seen of us.
       Therefore I have entreated him along
       With us to watch the minutes of this night,
       That, if again this apparition come,
       He may approve our eyes and speak to it.
   Horatio. Tush, tush, 'twill not appear.
30 *Bernardo.*   Sit down awhile,
       And let us once again assail your ears,
       That are so fortified against our story,
       What we two nights have seen.
   Horatio.   Well, sit we down,
       And let us hear Bernardo speak of this.
35 *Bernardo.* Last night of all,
       When yond same star that's westward from the pole
       Had made his course t' illume that part of heaven
       Where now it burns, Marcellus and myself,
       The bell then beating one —

   15 *Dane* King of Denmark   29 *approve* confirm   36 *pole* polestar

Enter Ghost.

Marcellus. Peace, break thee off. Look where it comes again. 40
Bernardo. In the same figure like the king that's dead.
Marcellus. Thou art a scholar; speak to it, Horatio.
Bernardo. Looks 'a not like the king? Mark it, Horatio.
Horatio. Most like. It harrows me with fear and wonder.
Bernardo. It would be spoke to.
Marcellus.   Speak to it, Horatio.   45
Horatio. What art thou that usurp'st this time of night
  Together with that fair and warlike form
  In which the majesty of buried Denmark
  Did sometimes march? By heaven I charge thee, speak.
Marcellus. It is offended.
Bernardo.   See, it stalks away.   50
Horatio. Stay. Speak, speak. I charge thee, speak.

                                              Exit Ghost.

Marcellus. 'Tis gone and will not answer.
Bernardo. How now, Horatio? You tremble and look pale.
  Is not this something more than fantasy?
  What think you on't?   55
Horatio. Before my God, I might not this believe
  Without the sensible and true avouch
  Of mine own eyes.
Marcellus.   Is it not like the king?
Horatio. As thou art to thyself.
  Such was the very armor he had on   60
  When he th' ambitious Norway combated.
  So frowned he once when, in an angry parle,
  He smote the sledded Polacks on the ice.
  'Tis strange.

48 *buried Denmark* the buried King of Denmark   49 *sometimes* formerly
61 *Norway* King of Norway   62 *parle* parley

65 *Marcellus.* Thus twice before, and jump at this dead hour,
     With martial stalk hath he gone by our watch.
     Horatio. In what particular thought to work I know not;
     But, in the gross and scope of my opinion,
     This bodes some strange eruption to our state.
     Marcellus. Good now, sit down, and tell me he that
70   knows,
     Why this same strict and most observant watch
     So nightly toils the subject of the land,
     And why such daily cast of brazen cannon
     And foreign mart for implements of war,
75 Why such impress of shipwrights, whose sore task
     Does not divide the Sunday from the week.
     What might be toward that this sweaty haste
     Doth make the night joint-laborer with the day?
     Who is't that can inform me?
     Horatio.   That can I.
80 At least the whisper goes so. Our last king,
     Whose image even but now appeared to us,
     Was as you know by Fortinbras of Norway,
     Thereto pricked on by a most emulate pride,
     Dared to the combat; in which our valiant Hamlet
85 (For so this side of our known world esteemed him)
     Did slay this Fortinbras; who, by a sealed compact
     Well ratified by law and heraldry,
     Did forfeit, with his life, all those his lands
     Which he stood seized of to the conqueror;
90 Against the which a moiety competent
     Was gagèd by our king, which had returned

65 *jump* just, exactly   68 *gross and scope* gross scope, general view   72 *toils* makes toil   *subject* subjects   74 *mart* trading   75 *impress* conscription 77 *toward* in preparation   83 *emulate* jealously rivalling   87 *law and heraldry* law of heralds regulating combat   89 *seized* possessed   90 *moiety competent* sufficient portion   91 *gagèd* engaged, staked

To the inheritance of Fortinbras
Had he been vanquisher, as, by the same comart
And carriage of the article designed,
His fell to Hamlet. Now, sir, young Fortinbras,   95
Of unimprovèd mettle hot and full,
Hath in the skirts of Norway here and there
Sharked up a list of lawless resolutes
For food and diet to some enterprise
That hath a stomach in't; which is no other,   100
As it doth well appear unto our state,
But to recover of us by strong hand
And terms compulsatory those foresaid lands
So by his father lost; and this, I take it,
Is the main motive of our preparations,   105
The source of this our watch, and the chief head
Of this posthaste and romage in the land.
Bernardo. I think it be no other but e'en so.
Well may it sort that this portentous figure
Comes armèd through our watch so like the king   110
That was and is the question of these wars.
Horatio. A mote it is to trouble the mind's eye.
In the most high and palmy state of Rome,
A little ere the mightiest Julius fell,
The graves stood tenantless and the sheeted dead   115
Did squeak and gibber in the Roman streets;
As stars with trains of fire and dews of blood,
Disasters in the sun; and the moist star
Upon whose influence Neptune's empire stands

93 *comart* joint bargain   94 *carriage* purport   96 *unimprovèd* unused
98 *Sharked* snatched indiscriminately as the shark takes prey   *resolutes*
desperadoes   100 *stomach* show of venturesomeness   106 *head* fountain-
head, source   107 *romage* intense activity   109 *sort* suit   112 *mote* speck of
dust   115 *sheeted* in shrouds   117 *As* (see Supplementary Notes, p. 175)
118 *Disasters* ominous signs   *moist star* moon

120   Was sick almost to doomsday with eclipse.
      And even the like precurse of feared events,
      As harbingers preceding still the fates
      And prologue to the omen coming on,
      Have heaven and earth together demonstrated
125   Unto our climatures and countrymen.

                        Enter Ghost.

      But soft, behold, lo where it comes again!
      I'll cross it, though it blast me. — Stay, illusion.
                                He spreads his arms.
      If thou hast any sound or use of voice,
      Speak to me.
130   If there be any good thing to be done
      That may to thee do ease and grace to me,
      Speak to me.
      If thou art privy to thy country's fate,
      Which happily foreknowing may avoid,
135   O, speak!
      Or if thou hast uphoarded in thy life
      Extorted treasure in the womb of earth,
      For which, they say, you spirits oft walk in death,
                                       The cock crows.
      Speak of it. Stay and speak. Stop it, Marcellus.
140 *Marcellus.* Shall I strike at it with my partisan?
    Horatio. Do, if it will not stand.
    Bernardo.   'Tis here.
    Horatio.   'Tis here.
    Marcellus. 'Tis gone.   *[Exit Ghost.]*
      We do it wrong, being so majestical,

121 *precurse* foreshadowing   122 *harbingers* forerunners   *still* constantly
123 *omen* calamity   125 *climatures* regions   127 *cross it* cross its path
134 *happily* haply, perchance   140 *partisan* pike

32

To offer it the show of violence,
For it is as the air invulnerable,   145
And our vain blows malicious mockery.
Bernardo. It was about to speak when the cock crew.
Horatio. And then it started, like a guilty thing
Upon a fearful summons. I have heard
The cock, that is the trumpet to the morn,   150
Doth with his lofty and shrill-sounding throat
Awake the god of day, and at his warning,
Whether in sea or fire, in earth or air,
Th' extravagant and erring spirit hies
To his confine; and of the truth herein   155
This present object made probation.
Marcellus. It faded on the crowing of the cock.
Some say that ever 'gainst that season comes
Wherein our Saviour's birth is celebrated,
This bird of dawning singeth all night long,   160
And then, they say, no spirit dare stir abroad,
The nights are wholesome, then no planets strike,
No fairy takes, nor witch hath power to charm.
So hallowed and so gracious is that time.
Horatio. So have I heard and do in part believe it.   165
But look, the morn in russet mantle clad
Walks o'er the dew of yon high eastward hill.
Break we our watch up, and by my advice
Let us impart what we have seen to-night
Unto young Hamlet, for upon my life   170
This spirit, dumb to us, will speak to him.
Do you consent we shall acquaint him with it,
As needful in our loves, fitting our duty?

154 *extravagant* wandering beyond bounds   *erring* wandering   156 *probation* proof   158 *'gainst* just before   162 *strike* work evil by influence   163 *takes* bewitches

Marcellus. Let's do't, I pray, and I this morning know
175   Where we shall find him most conveniently.   *Exeunt.*

❈

I, ii   *Flourish. Enter Claudius, King of Denmark, Gertrude the*
         Queen, Councillors, Polonius and his son Laertes, Ham-
         let, cum aliis [including Voltemand and Cornelius].

King. Though yet of Hamlet our dear brother's death
      The memory be green, and that it us befitted
      To bear our hearts in grief, and our whole kingdom
      To be contracted in one brow of woe,
5   Yet so far hath discretion fought with nature
      That we with wisest sorrow think on him
      Together with remembrance of ourselves.
      Therefore our sometime sister, now our queen,
      Th' imperial jointress to this warlike state,
10   Have we, as 'twere with a defeated joy,
      With an auspicious and a dropping eye,
      With mirth in funeral and with dirge in marriage,
      In equal scale weighing delight and dole,
      Taken to wife. Nor have we herein barred
15   Your better wisdoms, which have freely gone
      With this affair along. For all, our thanks.
      Now follows, that you know, young Fortinbras,
      Holding a weak supposal of our worth,
      Or thinking by our late dear brother's death
20   Our state to be disjoint and out of frame,

I, ii, s.d. *cum aliis* with others   9 *jointress* a woman who has a jointure, or
joint tenancy of an estate   14 *barred* excluded

Colleaguèd with this dream of his advantage,
He hath not failed to pester us with message
Importing the surrender of those lands
Lost by his father, with all bands of law,
To our most valiant brother. So much for him.   25
Now for ourself and for this time of meeting.
Thus much the business is: we have here writ
To Norway, uncle of young Fortinbras —
Who, impotent and bedrid, scarcely hears
Of this his nephew's purpose — to suppress   30
His further gait herein, in that the levies,
The lists, and full proportions are all made
Out of his subject; and we here dispatch
You, good Cornelius, and you, Voltemand,
For bearers of this greeting to old Norway,   35
Giving to you no further personal power
To business with the king, more than the scope
Of these delated articles allow.
Farewell, and let your haste commend your duty.
Cornelius, Voltemand. In that, and all things, will we show
    our duty.   40
King. We doubt it nothing. Heartily farewell.
                    [Exeunt Voltemand and Cornelius.]
And now, Laertes, what's the news with you?
You told us of some suit. What is't, Laertes?
You cannot speak of reason to the Dane
And lose your voice. What wouldst thou beg, Laertes,   45
That shall not be my offer, not thy asking?
The head is not more native to the heart,
The hand more instrumental to the mouth,

21 *Colleaguèd* united   **31** *gait* going   **32** *proportions* amounts of forces and
supplies   **38** *delated* detailed   **44** *Dane* King of Denmark   **45** *lose your*
voice speak in vain   **47** *native* joined by nature   **48** *instrumental* serviceable

Than is the throne of Denmark to thy father.
What wouldst thou have, Laertes?

50 *Laertes.*   My dread lord,
Your leave and favor to return to France,
From whence though willingly I came to Denmark
To show my duty in your coronation,
Yet now I must confess, that duty done,

55 My thoughts and wishes bend again toward France
And bow them to your gracious leave and pardon.

King. Have you your father's leave? What says Polonius?

Polonius. He hath, my lord, wrung from me my slow **leave**
By laborsome petition, and at last

60 Upon his will I sealed my hard consent.
I do beseech you give him leave to go.

King. Take thy fair hour, Laertes. Time be thine,
And thy best graces spend it at thy will.
But now, my cousin Hamlet, and my son —

65 *Hamlet.* [*aside*] A little more than kin, and less than kind!

King. How is it that the clouds still hang on you?

Hamlet. Not so, my lord. I am too much in the sun.

Queen. Good Hamlet, cast thy nighted color off,
And let thine eye look like a friend on Denmark.

70 Do not for ever with thy vailèd lids
Seek for thy noble father in the dust.
Thou know'st 'tis common. All that lives must die,
Passing through nature to eternity.

Hamlet. Ay, madam, it is common.

Queen.   If it be,

75 Why seems it so particular with thee?

64 *cousin* kinsman more distant than parent, child, brother, or sister
65 *kin* related as nephew *kind* kindly in feeling, as by kind, or nature,
a son would be to his father 67 *sun* sunshine of the king's undesired
favor (with the punning additional meaning of 'place of a son') 70 *vailed*
downcast

Hamlet. Seems, madam? Nay, it is. I know not 'seems.'
  'Tis not alone my inky cloak, good mother,
  Nor customary suits of solemn black,
  Nor windy suspiration of forced breath,
  No, nor the fruitful river in the eye,   80
  Nor the dejected havior of the visage,
  Together with all forms, moods, shapes of grief,
  That can denote me truly. These indeed seem,
  For they are actions that a man might play,
  But I have that within which passeth show —   85
  These but the trappings and the suits of woe.

King. 'Tis sweet and commendable in your nature, Hamlet,
  To give these mourning duties to your father,
  But you must know your father lost a father,
  That father lost, lost his, and the survivor bound   90
  In filial obligation for some term
  To do obsequious sorrow. But to persever
  In obstinate condolement is a course
  Of impious stubbornness. 'Tis unmanly grief.
  It shows a will most incorrect to heaven,   95
  A heart unfortified, a mind impatient,
  An understanding simple and unschooled.
  For what we know must be and is as common
  As any the most vulgar thing to sense,
  Why should we in our peevish opposition   100
  Take it to heart? Fie, 'tis a fault to heaven,
  A fault against the dead, a fault to nature,
  To reason most absurd, whose common theme
  Is death of fathers, and who still hath cried,
  From the first corse till he that died to-day,   105
  'This must be so.' We pray you throw to earth

92 *obsequious* proper to obsequies or funerals *persever* persevere (accented
on the second syllable, as always in Shakespeare)

This unprevailing woe, and think of us
As of a father, for let the world take note
You are the most immediate to our throne,
110   And with no less nobility of love
Than that which dearest father bears his son
Do I impart toward you. For your intent
In going back to school in Wittenberg,
It is most retrograde to our desire,
115   And we beseech you, bend you to remain
Here in the cheer and comfort of our eye,
Our chiefest courtier, cousin, and our son.
Queen. Let not thy mother lose her prayers, Hamlet.
I pray thee stay with us, go not to Wittenberg.
120 *Hamlet.* I shall in all my best obey you, madam.
King. Why, 'tis a loving and a fair reply.
Be as ourself in Denmark. Madam, come.
This gentle and unforced accord of Hamlet
Sits smiling to my heart, in grace whereof
125   No jocund health that Denmark drinks to-day
But the great cannon to the clouds shall tell,
And the king's rouse the heaven shall bruit again,
Respeaking earthly thunder. Come away.

Flourish. Exeunt all but Hamlet.

Hamlet. O that this too too sullied flesh would melt,
130   Thaw, and resolve itself into a dew,
Or that the Everlasting had not fixed
His canon 'gainst self-slaughter. O God, God,
How weary, stale, flat, and unprofitable
Seem to me all the uses of this world!
135   Fie on't, ah, fie, 'tis an unweeded garden
That grows to seed. Things rank and gross in nature

114 *retrograde* contrary 127 *rouse* toast drunk in wine *bruit* echo 129 *sullied* (see Supplementary Notes, p. 175) 132 *canon* law

38

Possess it merely. That it should come to this,
But two months dead, nay, not so much, not two,
So excellent a king, that was to this
Hyperion to a satyr, so loving to my mother   140
That he might not beteem the winds of heaven
Visit her face too roughly. Heaven and earth,
Must I remember? Why, she would hang on him
As if increase of appetite had grown
By what it fed on, and yet within a month —   145
Let me not think on't; frailty, thy name is woman —
A little month, or ere those shoes were old
With which she followed my poor father's body
Like Niobe, all tears, why she, even she —
O God, a beast that wants discourse of reason   150
Would have mourned longer — married with my uncle,
My father's brother, but no more like my father
Than I to Hercules. Within a month,
Ere yet the salt of most unrighteous tears
Had left the flushing in her gallèd eyes,   155
She married. O, most wicked speed, to post
With such dexterity to incestuous sheets!
It is not, nor it cannot come to good.
But break my heart, for I must hold my tongue.

Enter Horatio, Marcellus, and Bernardo.

Horatio. Hail to your lordship!
Hamlet.   I am glad to see you well.   160
    Horatio — or I do forget myself.

137 *merely* completely   140 *Hyperion* the sun god   141 *beteem* allow
149 *Niobe* the proud mother who boasted of having more children than
Leto and was punished when they were slain by Apollo and Artemis,
children of Leto; the grieving Niobe was changed by Zeus into a stone,
which continually dropped tears   150 *discourse* logical power or process
155 *gallèd* irritated

Horatio. The same, my lord, and your poor servant ever.

Hamlet. Sir, my good friend, I'll change that name with
you.

And what make you from Wittenberg, Horatio?

165   Marcellus?

Marcellus. My good lord!

Hamlet. I am very glad to see you. [*to Bernardo*] Good even,
sir.

But what, in faith, make you from Wittenberg?

Horatio. A truant disposition, good my lord.

170 *Hamlet.* I would not hear your enemy say so,
Nor shall you do my ear that violence
To make it truster of your own report
Against yourself. I know you are no truant.
But what is your affair in Elsinore?

175   We'll teach you to drink deep ere you depart.

Horatio. My lord, I came to see your father's funeral.

Hamlet. I prithee do not mock me, fellow student.
I think it was to see my mother's wedding.

Horatio. Indeed, my lord, it followed hard upon.

180 *Hamlet.* Thrift, thrift, Horatio. The funeral baked meats
Did coldly furnish forth the marriage tables.
Would I had met my dearest foe in heaven
Or ever I had seen that day, Horatio!
My father — methinks I see my father.

Horatio. Where, my lord?

185 *Hamlet.*   In my mind's eye, Horatio.

Horatio. I saw him once. 'A was a goodly king.

Hamlet. 'A was a man, take him for all in all,
I shall not look upon his like again.

Horatio. My lord, I think I saw him yesternight.

190 *Hamlet.* Saw? who?

163 *change* exchange   164 *make* do   182 *dearest* direst, bitterest

Horatio. My lord, the king your father.

Hamlet.   The king my father?

Horatio. Season your admiration for a while

   With an attent ear till I may deliver

   Upon the witness of these gentlemen

   This marvel to you.

Hamlet.   For God's love let me hear!   195

Horatio. Two nights together had these gentlemen,

   Marcellus and Bernardo, on their watch

   In the dead waste and middle of the night

   Been thus encountered. A figure like your father,

   Armèd at point exactly, cap-a-pe,   200

   Appears before them and with solemn march

   Goes slow and stately by them. Thrice he walked

   By their oppressed and fear-surprisèd eyes

   Within his truncheon's length, whilst they, distilled

   Almost to jelly with the act of fear,   205

   Stand dumb and speak not to him. This to me

   In dreadful secrecy impart they did,

   And I with them the third night kept the watch,

   Where, as they had delivered, both in time,

   Form of the thing, each word made true and good,   210

   The apparition comes. I knew your father.

   These hands are not more like.

Hamlet.   But where was this?

Marcellus. My lord, upon the platform where we watched.

Hamlet. Did you not speak to it?

Horatio.   My lord, I did,

   But answer made it none. Yet once methought   215

   It lifted up it head and did address

192 *Season your admiration* control your wonder 200 *at point* completely
cap-a-pe from head to foot 204 *truncheon* military commander's baton
216 *it* its

Itself to motion like as it would speak.
But even then the morning cock crew loud,
And at the sound it shrunk in haste away
And vanished from our sight.

220 *Hamlet.*   'Tis very strange.

Horatio. As I do live, my honored lord, 'tis true,
And we did think it writ down in our duty
To let you know of it.

Hamlet. Indeed, indeed, sirs, but this troubles me.
Hold you the watch to-night?

225 *All.*   We do, my lord.

Hamlet. Armed, say you?

All. Armed, my lord.

Hamlet. From top to toe?

All.   My lord, from head to foot.

Hamlet. Then saw you not his face?

230 *Horatio.* O, yes, my lord. He wore his beaver up.

Hamlet. What, looked he frowningly?

Horatio. A countenance more in sorrow than in anger.

Hamlet. Pale or red?

Horatio. Nay, very pale.

Hamlet.   And fixed his eyes upon you?

Horatio. Most constantly.

235 *Hamlet.*   I would I had been there.

Horatio. It would have much amazed you.

Hamlet. Very like, very like. Stayed it long?

Horatio. While one with moderate haste might tell a hundred.

Both. Longer, longer.

Horatio. Not when I saw't.

240 *Hamlet.*   His beard was grizzled, no?

230 *beaver* visor or movable face-guard of the helmet   238 *tell* count
240 *grizzled* grey

Horatio. It was as I have seen it in his life,
 A sable silvered.
Hamlet.   I will watch to-night.
 Perchance 'twill walk again.
Horatio.   I warr'nt it will.
Hamlet. If it assume my noble father's person,
 I'll speak to it though hell itself should gape   245
 And bid me hold my peace. I pray you all,
 If you have hitherto concealed this sight,
 Let it be tenable in your silence still,
 And whatsomever else shall hap to-night,
 Give it an understanding but no tongue.   250
 I will requite your loves. So fare you well.
 Upon the platform, 'twixt eleven and twelve
 I'll visit you.
All.   Our duty to your honor.
Hamlet. Your loves, as mine to you. Farewell.
                         Exeunt [all but Hamlet].
 My father's spirit — in arms? All is not well.   255
 I doubt some foul play. Would the night were come!
 Till then sit still, my soul. Foul deeds will rise,
 Though all the earth o'erwhelm them, to men's eyes.
                                                  Exit.

✣

          Enter Laertes and Ophelia, his sister.   I, iii

Laertes. My necessaries are embarked. Farewell.
 And, sister, as the winds give benefit

242 *sable silvered* black mixed with white   248 *tenable* held firmly
256 *doubt* suspect, fear

43

And convoy is assistant, do not sleep,
But let me hear from you.
Ophelia.   Do you doubt that?
5 *Laertes.* For Hamlet, and the trifling of his favor,
   Hold it a fashion and a toy in blood,
   A violet in the youth of primy nature,
   Forward, not permanent, sweet, not lasting,
   The perfume and suppliance of a minute,
   No more.
Ophelia.   No more but so?
10 *Laertes.*   Think it no more.
   For nature crescent does not grow alone
   In thews and bulk, but as this temple waxes
   The inward service of the mind and soul
   Grows wide withal. Perhaps he loves you now,
15 And now no soil nor cautel doth besmirch
   The virtue of his will, but you must fear,
   His greatness weighed, his will is not his own.
   [For he himself is subject to his birth.]
   He may not, as unvalued persons do,
20 Carve for himself, for on his choice depends
   The safety and health of this whole state,
   And therefore must his choice be circumscribed
   Unto the voice and yielding of that body
   Whereof he is the head. Then if he says he loves you,
25 It fits your wisdom so far to believe it
   As he in his particular act and place
   May give his saying deed, which is no further
   Than the main voice of Denmark goes withal.

I, iii, 3 *convoy* means of transport   7 *primy* of the springtime   9 *perfume
and suppliance* filling sweetness   11 *crescent* growing   12 *this temple* the
body   15 *cautel* deceit   16 *will* desire   17 *greatness weighed* high position
considered   23 *yielding* assent

Then weigh what loss your honor may sustain
If with too credent ear you list his songs,   30
Or lose your heart, or your chaste treasure open
To his unmastered importunity.
Fear it, Ophelia, fear it, my dear sister,
And keep you in the rear of your affection,
Out of the shot and danger of desire.   35
The chariest maid is prodigal enough
If she unmask her beauty to the moon.
Virtue itself scapes not calumnious strokes.
The canker galls the infants of the spring
Too oft before their buttons be disclosed,   40
And in the morn and liquid dew of youth
Contagious blastments are most imminent.
Be wary then; best safety lies in fear.
Youth to itself rebels, though none else near.
Ophelia. I shall the effect of this good lesson keep   45
As watchman to my heart, but, good my brother,
Do not as some ungracious pastors do,
Show me the steep and thorny way to heaven,
Whiles like a puffed and reckless libertine
Himself the primrose path of dalliance treads   50
And recks not his own rede.

Enter Polonius.

Laertes.   O, fear me not.
I stay too long. But here my father comes.
A double blessing is a double grace;
Occasion smiles upon a second leave.
Polonius. Yet here, Laertes? Aboard, aboard, for shame!   55

30 *credent* credulous 34 *affection* feelings, which rashly lead forward into
dangers 39 *canker* rose worm *galls* injures 40 *buttons* buds 42 *blastments* blights 51 *recks* regards *rede* counsel

45

The wind sits in the shoulder of your sail,
And you are stayed for. There—my blessing with
  thee,
And these few precepts in thy memory
Look thou character. Give thy thoughts no tongue,

60 Nor any unproportioned thought his act.
Be thou familiar, but by no means vulgar.
Those friends thou hast, and their adoption tried,
Grapple them unto thy soul with hoops of steel,
But do not dull thy palm with entertainment

65 Of each new-hatched, unfledged courage. Beware
Of entrance to a quarrel; but being in,
Bear't that th' opposèd may beware of thee.
Give every man thine ear, but few thy voice;
Take each man's censure, but reserve thy judgment.

70 Costly thy habit as thy purse can buy,
But not expressed in fancy; rich, not gaudy,
For the apparel oft proclaims the man,
And they in France of the best rank and station
Are of a most select and generous chief in that.

75 Neither a borrower nor a lender be,
For loan oft loses both itself and friend,
And borrowing dulleth edge of husbandry.
This above all, to thine own self be true,
And it must follow as the night the day

80 Thou canst not then be false to any man.
Farewell. My blessing season this in thee!
Laertes. Most humbly do I take my leave, my lord.
Polonius. The time invites you. Go, your servants tend.

---

59 *character* inscribe   60 *unproportioned* unadjusted to what is right
65 *courage* man of spirit, young blood   69 *censure* judgment   74 *chief*
eminence   77 *husbandry* thriftiness   81 *season* ripen and make fruitful
83 *tend* wait

Laertes. Farewell, Ophelia, and remember well
   What I have said to you.
Ophelia.   'Tis in my memory locked,   85
   And you yourself shall keep the key of it.
Laertes. Farewell.   *Exit Laertes.*
Polonius. What is't, Ophelia, he hath said to you?
Ophelia. So please you, something touching the Lord Ham-
   let.
Polonius. Marry, well bethought.   90
   'Tis told me he hath very oft of late
   Given private time to you, and you yourself
   Have of your audience been most free and bounteous.
   If it be so — as so 'tis put on me,
   And that in way of caution — I must tell you   95
   You do not understand yourself so clearly
   As it behooves my daughter and your honor.
   What is between you? Give me up the truth.
Ophelia. He hath, my lord, of late made many tenders
   Of his affection to me.   100
Polonius. Affection? Pooh! You speak like a green girl,
   Unsifted in such perilous circumstance.
   Do you believe his tenders, as you call them?
Ophelia. I do not know, my lord, what I should think.
Polonius. Marry, I will teach you. Think yourself a
   baby   105
   That you have ta'en these tenders for true pay

---

90 *Marry* by Mary 99 *tenders* offers 102 *Unsifted* untested 106–9 *tenders*
... *Tender* ... *tender* offers ... hold in regard ... present (a word play
going through three meanings, the last use of the word yielding further
complexity with its valid implications that she will show herself to him
as a fool, will show him to the world as a fool, and may go so far as to
present him with a baby, which would be a fool because 'fool' was an Elizabethan term of endearment especially applicable to an infant as a 'little
innocent')

47

Which are not sterling. Tender yourself more dearly,
Or (not to crack the wind of the poor phrase,
Running it thus) you'll tender me a fool.

110 *Ophelia.* My lord, he hath importuned me with love
In honorable fashion.

Polonius. Ay, fashion you may call it. Go to, go to.

Ophelia. And hath given countenance to his speech, my
lord,
With almost all the holy vows of heaven.

115 *Polonius.* Ay, springes to catch woodcocks. I do know,
When the blood burns, how prodigal the soul
Lends the tongue vows. These blazes, daughter,
Giving more light than heat, extinct in both
Even in their promise, as it is a-making,
120 You must not take for fire. From this time
Be something scanter of your maiden presence.
Set your entreatments at a higher rate
Than a command to parley. For Lord Hamlet,
Believe so much in him that he is young,
125 And with a larger tether may he walk
Than may be given you. In few, Ophelia,
Do not believe his vows, for they are brokers,
Not of that dye which their investments show,
But mere implorators of unholy suits,
130 Breathing like sanctified and pious bawds,
The better to beguile. This is for all:
I would not, in plain terms, from this time forth
Have you so slander any moment leisure

108 *crack . . . of* make wheeze like a horse driven too hard   112 *Go to*
go away, go on (expressing impatience)   115 *springes* snares   *woodcocks*
birds believed foolish   122 *entreatments* military negotiations for surrender   123 *parley* confer with a besieger   127 *brokers* middlemen, panders   128 *investments* clothes   133 *slander* use disgracefully   *moment*
momentary

As to give words or talk with the Lord Hamlet.
Look to't, I charge you. Come your ways.   135
Ophelia. I shall obey, my lord.   *Exeunt.*

❈

Enter Hamlet, Horatio, and Marcellus.   I, iv

Hamlet. The air bites shrewdly; it is very cold.
Horatio. It is a nipping and an eager air.
Hamlet. What hour now?
Horatio.   I think it lacks of twelve.
Marcellus. No, it is struck.
Horatio. Indeed? I heard it not. It then draws near the season 5
     Wherein the spirit held his wont to walk.
               A flourish of trumpets, and two pieces goes off.
     What does this mean, my lord?
Hamlet. The king doth wake to-night and takes his rouse,
     Keeps wassail, and the swaggering upspring reels,
     And as he drains his draughts of Rhenish down   10
     The kettledrum and trumpet thus bray out
     The triumph of his pledge.
Horatio.   Is it a custom?
Hamlet. Ay, marry, is't,
     But to my mind, though I am native here
     And to the manner born, it is a custom   15
     More honored in the breach than the observance.
     This heavy-headed revel east and west
     Makes us traduced and taxed of other nations.

I, iv, 1 *shrewdly* wickedly   2 *eager* sharp   8 *rouse* carousal   9 *upspring*
a German dance   10 *Rhenish* Rhine wine   12 *triumph* achievement, feat
(in downing a cup of wine at one draught)   16 *More . . . observance* better
broken than observed   18 *taxed of* censured by

They clepe us drunkards and with swinish phrase
20 Soil our addition, and indeed it takes
From our achievements, though performed at height,
The pith and marrow of our attribute.
So oft it chances in particular men
That (for some vicious mole of nature in them,
25 As in their birth, wherein they are not guilty,
Since nature cannot choose his origin)
By the o'ergrowth of some complexion,
Oft breaking down the pales and forts of reason,
Or by some habit that too much o'erleavens
30 The form of plausive manners — that (these men
Carrying, I say, the stamp of one defect,
Being nature's livery, or fortune's star)
Their virtues else, be they as pure as grace,
As infinite as man may undergo,
35 Shall in the general censure take corruption
From that particular fault. The dram of evil
Doth all the noble substance of a doubt,
To his own scandal.

Enter Ghost.

Horatio.   Look, my lord, it comes.
Hamlet. Angels and ministers of grace defend us!
40 Be thou a spirit of health or goblin damned,
Bring with thee airs from heaven or blasts from hell,
Be thy intents wicked or charitable,

19 *clepe* call   20 *addition* reputation, title added as a distinction   22 *attri-bute* reputation, what is attributed   24 *mole* blemish, flaw   26 *his* its   27 *complexion* part of the make-up, combination of humors   28 *pales* bar-riers, fences   29 *o'erleavens* works change throughout, as yeast ferments dough   30 *plausive* pleasing   32 *livery* characteristic equipment or pro-vision   *star* make-up as formed by stellar influence   37 *Doth . . . doubt* (see Supplementary Notes, p. 175)   40 *of health* sound, good   *goblin* fiend

Thou com'st in such a questionable shape
That I will speak to thee. I'll call thee Hamlet,
King, father, royal Dane. O, answer me!   45
Let me not burst in ignorance, but tell
Why thy canonized bones, hearsèd in death,
Have burst their cerements, why the sepulchre
Wherein we saw thee quietly interred
Hath oped his ponderous and marble jaws   50
To cast thee up again. What may this mean
That thou, dead corse, again in complete steel,
Revisits thus the glimpses of the moon,
Making night hideous, and we fools of nature
So horridly to shake our disposition   55
With thoughts beyond the reaches of our souls?
Say, why is this? wherefore? what should we do?
                                        [Ghost] beckons.

Horatio. It beckons you to go away with it,
    As if it some impartment did desire
    To you alone.
Marcellus.   Look with what courteous action   60
    It waves you to a more removèd ground.
    But do not go with it.
Horatio.   No, by no means.
Hamlet. It will not speak. Then will I follow it.
Horatio. Do not, my lord.
Hamlet.   Why, what should be the fear?
    I do not set my life at a pin's fee,   65
    And for my soul, what can it do to that,
    Being a thing immortal as itself?
    It waves me forth again. I'll follow it.

47 *canonized* buried with the established rites of the Church 48 *cerements*
waxed grave-cloths 54 *fools of nature* men made conscious of natural
limitations by a supernatural manifestation

Horatio. What if it tempt you toward the flood, my lord,
70   Or to the dreadful summit of the cliff
That beetles o'er his base into the sea,
And there assume some other horrible form,
Which might deprive your sovereignty of reason
And draw you into madness? Think of it.
75   The very place puts toys of desperation,
Without more motive, into every brain
That looks so many fathoms to the sea
And hears it roar beneath.

Hamlet.   It waves me still.
Go on. I'll follow thee.

Marcellus. You shall not go, my lord.

80 *Hamlet.*   **Hold off your hands.**

Horatio. Be ruled. You shall not go.

Hamlet.   My fate cries out
And makes each petty artere in this body
As hardy as the Nemean lion's nerve.
Still am I called. Unhand me, gentlemen.
85   By heaven, I'll make a ghost of him that lets me!
I say, away! Go on. I'll follow thee.

                         Exit Ghost, and Hamlet.

Horatio. He waxes desperate with imagination.

Marcellus. Let's follow. 'Tis not fit thus to obey him.

Horatio. Have after. To what issue will this come?

90 *Marcellus.* Something is rotten in the state of Denmark.

Horatio. Heaven will direct it.

Marcellus.   Nay, let's follow him.   *Exeunt.*

❁

71 *beetles* juts out   73 *deprive* take away   *sovereignty of reason* state of
being ruled by reason   75 *toys* fancies   82 *artere* artery   83 *Nemean lion*
a lion slain by Hercules in the performance of one of his twelve labors
nerve sinew   85 *lets* hinders

Enter Ghost and Hamlet.   I, v

Hamlet. Whither wilt thou lead me? Speak. I'll go no
    further.
Ghost. Mark me.
Hamlet.   I will.
Ghost.   My hour is almost come,
    When I to sulph'rous and tormenting flames
    Must render up myself.
Hamlet.   Alas, poor ghost!
Ghost. Pity me not, but lend thy serious hearing   5
    To what I shall unfold.
Hamlet.   Speak. I am bound to hear.
Ghost. So art thou to revenge, when thou shalt hear.
Hamlet. What?
Ghost. I am thy father's spirit,
    Doomed for a certain term to walk the night,   10
    And for the day confined to fast in fires,
    Till the foul crimes done in my days of nature
    Are burnt and purged away. But that I am forbid
    To tell the secrets of my prison house,
    I could a tale unfold whose lightest word   15
    Would harrow up thy soul, freeze thy young blood,
    Make thy two eyes like stars start from their spheres,
    Thy knotted and combinèd locks to part,
    And each particular hair to stand an end
    Like quills upon the fretful porpentine.   20
    But this eternal blazon must not be
    To ears of flesh and blood. List, list, O, list!
    If thou didst ever thy dear father love —

I, v, 3 *flames* sufferings in purgatory (not hell)   11 *fast* do penance
17 *spheres* transparent revolving shells in each of which, according to
the Ptolemaic astronomy, a planet or other heavenly body was placed
19 *an* on   20 *porpentine* porcupine   21 *eternal blazon* revelation of eternity

Hamlet. O God!

25 *Ghost.* Revenge his foul and most unnatural murther.

Hamlet. Murther?

Ghost. Murther most foul, as in the best it is,
But this most foul, strange, and unnatural.

Hamlet. Haste me to know't, that I, with wings as swift

30   As meditation or the thoughts of love,
May sweep to my revenge.

Ghost.   I find thee apt,
And duller shouldst thou be than the fat weed
That roots itself in ease on Lethe wharf,
Wouldst thou not stir in this. Now, Hamlet, hear.

85   'Tis given out that, sleeping in my orchard,
A serpent stung me. So the whole ear of Denmark
Is by a forgèd process of my death
Rankly abused. But know, thou noble youth,
The serpent that did sting thy father's life
Now wears his crown.

40 *Hamlet.*   O my prophetic soul!
My uncle?

Ghost. Ay, that incestuous, that adulterate beast,
With witchcraft of his wit, with traitorous gifts —
O wicked wit and gifts, that have the power

45   So to seduce! — won to his shameful lust
The will of my most seeming-virtuous queen.
O Hamlet, what a falling-off was there,
From me, whose love was of that dignity
That it went hand in hand even with the vow

50   I made to her in marriage, and to decline
Upon a wretch whose natural gifts were poor

---

30 *meditation* thought   33 *Lethe* the river in Hades which brings forgetfulness of past life to a spirit who drinks of it   37 *forgèd process* falsified
official report   42 *adulterate* adulterous

To those of mine!
But virtue, as it never will be moved,
Though lewdness court it in a shape of heaven,
So lust, though to a radiant angel linked,   55
Will sate itself in a celestial bed
And prey on garbage.
But soft, methinks I scent the morning air.
Brief let me be. Sleeping within my orchard,
My custom always of the afternoon,   60
Upon my secure hour thy uncle stole
With juice of cursed hebona in a vial,
And in the porches of my ears did pour
The leperous distilment, whose effect
Holds such an enmity with blood of man   65
That swift as quicksilver it courses through
The natural gates and alleys of the body,
And with a sudden vigor it doth posset
And curd, like eager droppings into milk,
The thin and wholesome blood. So did it mine,   70
And a most instant tetter barked about
Most lazar-like with vile and loathsome crust
All my smooth body.
Thus was I sleeping by a brother's hand
Of life, of crown, of queen at once dispatched,   75
Cut off even in the blossoms of my sin,
Unhouseled, disappointed, unaneled,
No reck'ning made, but sent to my account
With all my imperfections on my head.
O, horrible! O, horrible! most horrible!   80

54 *shape of heaven* angelic disguise   61 *secure* carefree, unsuspecting
62 *hebona* some poisonous plant   68 *posset* curdle   69 *eager* sour   71 *tetter* eruption   *barked* covered as with a bark   72 *lazar-like* leper-like
77 *Unhouseled* without the Sacrament   *disappointed* unprepared spiritually
unaneled without extreme unction

If thou hast nature in thee, bear it not.
Let not the royal bed of Denmark be
A couch for luxury and damnèd incest.
But howsomever thou pursues this act,
85 Taint not thy mind, nor let thy soul contrive
Against thy mother aught. Leave her to heaven
And to those thorns that in her bosom lodge
To prick and sting her. Fare thee well at once.
The glowworm shows the matin to be near
90 And gins to pale his uneffectual fire.
Adieu, adieu, adieu. Remember me.   *[Exit.]*
Hamlet. O all you host of heaven! O earth! What else?
And shall I couple hell? O fie! Hold, hold, my heart,
And you, my sinews, grow not instant old,
95 But bear me stiffly up. Remember thee?
Ay, thou poor ghost, while memory holds a seat
In this distracted globe. Remember thee?
Yea, from the table of my memory
I'll wipe away all trivial fond records,
100 All saws of books, all forms, all pressures past
That youth and observation copied there,
And thy commandment all alone shall live
Within the book and volume of my brain,
Unmixed with baser matter. Yes, by heaven!
105 O most pernicious woman!
O villain, villain, smiling, damnèd villain!
My tables — meet it is I set it down
That one may smile, and smile, and be a villain.
At least I am sure it may be so in Denmark.   *[Writes.]*

---

83 *luxury* lust 89 *matin* morning 97 *globe* head 98 *table* writing tablet,
record book 100 *saws* wise sayings *forms* mental images, concepts *pressures* impressions

So, uncle, there you are. Now to my word: 110
It is 'Adieu, adieu, remember me.'
I have sworn't.

Enter Horatio and Marcellus.

Horatio. My lord, my lord!
Marcellus.   Lord Hamlet!
Horatio.   Heavens secure him!
Hamlet. So be it!
Marcellus. Illo, ho, ho, my lord!   115
Hamlet. Hillo, ho, ho, boy! Come, bird, come.
Marcellus. How is't, my noble lord?
Horatio.   What news, my lord?
Hamlet. O, wonderful!
Horatio. Good my lord, tell it.
Hamlet.   No, you will reveal it.
Horatio. Not I, my lord, by heaven.
Marcellus.   Nor I, my lord.   120
Hamlet. How say you then? Would heart of man once think
    it?
    But you'll be secret?
Both.   Ay, by heaven, my lord.
Hamlet. There's never a villain dwelling in all Denmark
    But he's an arrant knave.
Horatio. There needs no ghost, my lord, come from the
    grave   125
    To tell us this.
Hamlet.   Why, right, you are in the right,
    And so, without more circumstance at all,
    I hold it fit that we shake hands and part:
    You, as your business and desires shall point you,

115 *Illo, ho, ho* cry of the falconer to summon his hawk   127 *circumstance*
ceremony

130   For every man hath business and desire
      Such as it is, and for my own poor part,
      Look you, I'll go pray.

Horatio. These are but wild and whirling words, **my lord.**

Hamlet. I am sorry they offend you, heartily;
      Yes, faith, heartily.

135 *Horatio.*   There's no offense, my lord.

Hamlet. Yes, by Saint Patrick, but there is, Horatio,
      And much offense too. Touching this vision here,
      It is an honest ghost, that let me tell you.
      For your desire to know what is between us,

140   O'ermaster't as you may. And now, good friends,
      As you are friends, scholars, and soldiers,
      Give me one poor request.

Horatio. What is't, my lord? We will.

Hamlet. Never make known what you have seen to-night.

Both. My lord, we will not.

Hamlet.   Nay, but swear't.

145 *Horatio.*   In faith,
      My lord, not I.

Marcellus.   Nor I, my lord — in faith.

Hamlet. Upon my sword.

Marcellus.   We have sworn, my lord, already.

Hamlet. Indeed, upon my sword, indeed.

                         Ghost cries under the stage.

Ghost. Swear.

Hamlet. Ha, ha, boy, say'st thou so? Art thou there, true-
150   penny?
      Come on. You hear this fellow in the cellarage.
      Consent to swear.

Horatio.   Propose the oath, my lord.

---

138 *honest* genuine (not a disguised demon)   147 *sword* i.e. upon the cross formed by the sword hilt   150 *truepenny* honest old fellow

Hamlet. Never to speak of this that you have seen,
  Swear by my sword.
Ghost. [*beneath*] Swear.   155
Hamlet. Hic et ubique? Then we'll shift our ground.
  Come hither, gentlemen,
  And lay your hands again upon my sword.
  Swear by my sword
  Never to speak of this that you have heard.   160
Ghost. [*beneath*] Swear by his sword.
Hamlet. Well said, old mole! Canst work i' th' earth so fast?
  A worthy pioner! Once more remove, good friends.
Horatio. O day and night, but this is wondrous strange!
Hamlet. And therefore as a stranger give it welcome.   165
  There are more things in heaven and earth, Horatio,
  Than are dreamt of in your philosophy.
  But come:
  Here as before, never, so help you mercy,
  How strange or odd some'er I bear myself   170
  (As I perchance hereafter shall think meet
  To put an antic disposition on),
  That you, at such times seeing me, never shall,
  With arms encumb'red thus, or this head-shake,
  Or by pronouncing of some doubtful phrase,   175
  As 'Well, well, we know,' or 'We could, an if we would,'
  Or 'If we list to speak,' or 'There be, an if they might,'
  Or such ambiguous giving out, to note
  That you know aught of me — this do swear,
  So grace and mercy at your most need help you.   180
Ghost. [*beneath*] Swear.   [*They swear.*]
Hamlet. Rest, rest, perturbèd spirit! So, gentlemen,

156 *Hic et ubique* here and everywhere 163 *pioner* pioneer, miner 167 *your philosophy* this philosophy one hears about 172 *antic* grotesque, mad 174 *encumb'red* folded 176 *an if* if

With all my love I do commend me to you,
And what so poor a man as Hamlet is
185 May do t' express his love and friending to you,
God willing, shall not lack. Let us go in together,
And still your fingers on your lips, I pray.
The time is out of joint. O cursèd spite
That ever I was born to set it right!
190 Nay, come, let's go together. *Exeunt.*

❖

II, i   *Enter old Polonius, with his man [Reynaldo].*

Polonius. Give him this money and these notes, Reynaldo.
Reynaldo. I will, my lord.
Polonius. You shall do marvellous wisely, good Reynaldo,
  Before you visit him, to make inquire
  Of his behavior.
5 *Reynaldo.*   My lord, I did intend it.
Polonius. Marry, well said, very well said. Look you, sir,
  Enquire me first what Danskers are in Paris,
  And how, and who, what means, and where they keep,
  What company, at what expense; and finding
10 By this encompassment and drift of question
  That they do know my son, come you more nearer
  Than your particular demands will touch it.
  Take you as 'twere some distant knowledge of him,
  As thus, 'I know his father and his friends,
15 And in part him' — do you mark this, Reynaldo?
Reynaldo. Ay, very well, my lord.

---

183 *commend* entrust 187 *still* always II, i, 7 *Danskers* Danes 8 *what
means* what their wealth *keep* dwell 10 *encompassment* circling about
12 *particular demands* definite questions

Polonius. 'And in part him, but,' you may say, 'not well,
    But if't be he I mean, he's very wild
    Addicted so and so.' And there put on him
    What forgeries you please; marry, none so rank   20
    As may dishonor him – take heed of that –
    But, sir, such wanton, wild, and usual slips
    As are companions noted and most known
    To youth and liberty.
Reynaldo.   As gaming, my lord.
Polonius. Ay, or drinking, fencing, swearing, quarrelling, 25
    Drabbing. You may go so far.
Reynaldo. My lord, that would dishonor him.
Polonius. Faith, no, as you may season it in the charge.
    You must not put another scandal on him,
    That he is open to incontinency.   30
    That's not my meaning. But breathe his faults so quaintly
    That they may seem the taints of liberty,
    The flash and outbreak of a fiery mind,
    A savageness in unreclaimèd blood,
    Of general assault.
Reynaldo.   But, my good lord –   35
Polonius. Wherefore should you do this?
Reynaldo.   Ay, my lord,
    I would know that.
Polonius.   Marry, sir, here's my drift,
    And I believe it is a fetch of warrant.
    You laying these slight sullies on my son
    As 'twere a thing a little soiled i' th' working,   40
    Mark you,

20 *forgeries* invented wrongdoings   26 *Drabbing* whoring   28 *season* soften   30 *incontinency* extreme sensuality   31 *quaintly* expertly, gracefully 34 *unreclaimèd* untamed   35 *Of general assault* assailing all young men 38 *fetch of warrant* allowable trick

Your party in converse, him you would sound,
Having ever seen in the prenominate crimes
The youth you breathe of guilty, be assured
45 He closes with you in this consequence:
'Good sir,' or so, or 'friend,' or 'gentleman' –
According to the phrase or the addition
Of man and country –
Reynaldo.   Very good, my lord.
Polonius. And then, sir, does 'a this – 'a does –
50 What was I about to say? By the mass, I was about to say
something! Where did I leave?
Reynaldo. At 'closes in the consequence,' at 'friend or so,'
and 'gentleman.'
Polonius. At 'closes in the consequence' – Ay, marry!
55 He closes thus: 'I know the gentleman;
I saw him yesterday, or t'other day,
Or then, or then, with such or such, and, as you say,
There was 'a gaming, there o'ertook in's rouse,
There falling out at tennis'; or perchance,
60 'I saw him enter such a house of sale,'
Videlicet, a brothel, or so forth.
See you now –
Your bait of falsehood takes this carp of truth,
And thus do we of wisdom and of reach,
65 With windlasses and with assays of bias,
By indirections find directions out.
So, by my former lecture and advice,
Shall you my son. You have me, have you not?

43 *Having ever* if he has ever *prenominate* aforementioned 45 *closes with
you* follows your lead to a conclusion *consequence* following way 47 *addition* title 58 *o'ertook* overcome with drunkenness *rouse* carousal
59 *falling out* quarrelling 61 *Videlicet* namely 64 *reach* far-reaching comprehension 65 *windlasses* roundabout courses *assays of bias* devious attacks 66 *directions* ways of procedure

Reynaldo. My lord, I have.
Polonius.   God bye ye, fare ye well.
Reynaldo. Good my lord.   70
Polonius. Observe his inclination in yourself.
Reynaldo. I shall, my lord.
Polonius. And let him ply his music.
Reynaldo.   Well, my lord.
Polonius. Farewell.   *Exit Reynaldo.*

Enter Ophelia.

                    How now, Ophelia, what's the matter?
Ophelia. O my lord, my lord, I have been so affrighted!   75
Polonius. With what, i' th' name of God?
Ophelia. My lord, as I was sewing in my closet,
    Lord Hamlet, with his doublet all unbraced,
    No hat upon his head, his stockings fouled,
    Ungartered, and down-gyvèd to his ankle,   80
    Pale as his shirt, his knees knocking each other,
    And with a look so piteous in purport
    As if he had been loosèd out of hell
    To speak of horrors — he comes before me.
Polonius. Mad for thy love?
Ophelia.   My lord, I do not know,   85
    But truly I do fear it.
Polonius.   What said he?
Ophelia. He took me by the wrist and held me hard.
    Then goes he to the length of all his arm,
    And with his other hand thus o'er his brow
    He falls to such perusal of my face   90
    As 'a would draw it. Long stayed he so.

69 *God bye ye* God be with you, good-bye   77 *closet* private living-room
78 *doublet* jacket   *unbraced* unlaced   80 *down-gyvèd* fallen down like gyves
or fetters on a prisoner's legs

At last, a little shaking of mine arm
And thrice his head thus waving up and down,
He raised a sigh so piteous and profound
95 As it did seem to shatter all his bulk
And end his being. That done, he lets me go,
And with his head over his shoulder turned
He seemed to find his way without his eyes,
For out o' doors he went without their helps
100 And to the last bended their light on me.
Polonius. Come, go with me. I will go seek the king.
This is the very ecstasy of love,
Whose violent property fordoes itself
And leads the will to desperate undertakings
105 As oft as any passion under heaven
That does afflict our natures. I am sorry.
What, have you given him any hard words of late?
Ophelia. No, my good lord; but as you did command
I did repel his letters and denied
His access to me.
110 *Polonius.*   That hath made him mad.
I am sorry that with better heed and judgment
I had not quoted him. I feared he did but trifle
And meant to wrack thee; but beshrew my jealousy.
By heaven, it is as proper to our age
115 To cast beyond ourselves in our opinions
As it is common for the younger sort
To lack discretion. Come, go we to the king.
This must be known, which, being kept close, might
move

---

102 *ecstasy* madness   103 *property* quality   *fordoes* destroys   112 *quoted* observed   113 *beshrew* curse   115 *cast beyond ourselves* find by calculation more significance in something than we ought to   118 *close* secret   *move* cause

More grief to hide than hate to utter love.
Come.   *Exeunt.* 120

❀

Flourish. Enter King and Queen, Rosencrantz, and Guil-   II, ii
    denstern [with others].

King. Welcome, dear Rosencrantz and Guildenstern.
    Moreover that we much did long to see you,
    The need we have to use you did provoke
    Our hasty sending. Something have you heard
    Of Hamlet's transformation — so call it,   5
    Sith nor th' exterior nor the inward man
    Resembles that it was. What it should be,
    More than his father's death, that thus hath put him
    So much from th' understanding of himself,
    I cannot dream of. I entreat you both   10
    That, being of so young days brought up with him,
    And sith so neighbored to his youth and havior,
    That you vouchsafe your rest here in our court
    Some little time, so by your companies
    To draw him on to pleasures, and to gather   15
    So much as from occasion you may glean,
    Whether aught to us unknown afflicts him thus,
    That opened lies within our remedy.
Queen. Good gentlemen, he hath much talked of you,
    And sure I am two men there are not living   20

119 *to hide . . . love* by such hiding of love than there would be hate
moved by a revelation of it (a violently condensed putting of the case
which is a triumph of special statement for Polonius) II, ii, 2 *Moreover
that* besides the fact that 6 *Sith* since 12 *youth and havior* youthful ways
of life 18 *opened* revealed

To whom he more adheres. If it will please you
To show us so much gentry and good will
As to expend your time with us awhile
For the supply and profit of our hope,
25   Your visitation shall receive such thanks
As fits a king's remembrance.

Rosencrantz.   Both your majesties
Might, by the sovereign power you have of us,
Put your dread pleasures more into command
Than to entreaty.

Guildenstern.   But we both obey,
30   And here give up ourselves in the full bent
To lay our service freely at your feet,
To be commanded.

King. Thanks, Rosencrantz and gentle Guildenstern.
Queen. Thanks, Guildenstern and gentle Rosencrantz.
35   And I beseech you instantly to visit
My too much changèd son. — Go, some of you,
And bring these gentlemen where Hamlet is.

Guildenstern. Heavens make our presence and our practices
Pleasant and helpful to him!

Queen.   Ay, amen!

        Exeunt Rosencrantz and Guildenstern,
            [with some Attendants].

Enter Polonius.

40 *Polonius.* Th' ambassadors from Norway, my good lord
Are joyfully returned.

King. Thou still hast been the father of good news.

Polonius. Have I, my lord? Assure you, my good liege,
I hold my duty as I hold my soul,

---

21 *more adheres* is more attached   22 *gentry* courtesy   30 *in the full bent*
at the limit of bending (of a bow), to full capacity   42 *still* always

Both to my God and to my gracious king, 45
And I do think — or else this brain of mine
Hunts not the trail of policy so sure
As it hath used to do — that I have found
The very cause of Hamlet's lunacy.
King. O, speak of that! That do I long to hear. 50
Polonius. Give first admittance to th' ambassadors.
My news shall be the fruit to that great feast.
King. Thyself do grace to them and bring them in.

[Exit Polonius.]

He tells me, my dear Gertrude, he hath found
The head and source of all your son's distemper. 55
Queen. I doubt it is no other but the main,
His father's death and our o'erhasty marriage.
King. Well, we shall sift him.

*Enter Ambassadors [(Voltemand and Cornelius), with
Polonius].*

Welcome, my good friends.
Say, Voltemand, what from our brother Norway?
Voltemand. Most fair return of greetings and desires. 60
Upon our first, he sent out to suppress
His nephew's levies, which to him appeared
To be a preparation 'gainst the Polack,
But better looked into, he truly found
It was against your highness, whereat grieved, 65
That so his sickness, age, and impotence
Was falsely borne in hand, sends out arrests
On Fortinbras; which he in brief obeys,
Receives rebuke from Norway, and in fine

52 *fruit* dessert   53 *grace* honor   56 *doubt* suspect   61 *our first* our first
words about the matter   67 *borne in hand* deceived   69 *in fine* in the end

70 Makes vow before his uncle never more
To give th' assay of arms against your majesty.
Whereon old Norway, overcome with joy,
Gives him threescore thousand crowns in annual fee
And his commission to employ those soldiers,
75 So levied as before, against the Polack,
With an entreaty, herein further shown, *[Gives a paper.]*
That it might please you to give quiet pass
Through your dominions for this enterprise,
On such regards of safety and allowance
As therein are set down.

80 *King.*   It likes us well;
And at our more considered time we'll read,
Answer, and think upon this business.
Meantime we thank you for your well-took labor.
Go to your rest; at night we'll feast together.
Most welcome home!   *Exeunt Ambassadors.*

85 *Polonius.*   This business is well ended.
My liege and madam, to expostulate
What majesty should be, what duty is,
Why day is day, night night, and time is time,
Were nothing but to waste night, day, and time.
90 Therefore, since brevity is the soul of wit,
And tediousness the limbs and outward flourishes,
I will be brief. Your noble son is mad.
Mad call I it, for, to define true madness,
What is't but to be nothing else but mad?
But let that go.

95 *Queen.*   More matter, with less art.
Polonius. Madam, I swear I use no art at all.
That he is mad, 'tis true: 'tis true 'tis pity,

71 assay trial   79 *regards* terms   81 *considered time* convenient time for consideration   86 *expostulate* discuss   90 *wit* understanding

And pity 'tis 'tis true — a foolish figure.
But farewell it, for I will use no art.
Mad let us grant him then, and now remains   100
That we find out the cause of this effect
Or rather say, the cause of this defect,
For this effect defective comes by cause.
Thus it remains, and the remainder thus.
Perpend.   105
I have a daughter (have while she is mine),
Who in her duty and obedience, mark,
Hath given me this. Now gather, and surmise.

[Reads the] letter.
'To the celestial, and my soul's idol, the most beautified
Ophelia,' —   110
That's an ill phrase, a vile phrase; 'beautified' is a vile
phrase. But you shall hear. Thus: *[Reads.*
'In her excellent white bosom, these, &c.'
Queen. Came this from Hamlet to her?
Polonius. Good madam, stay awhile. I will be faithful.   115
[Reads.]

'Doubt thou the stars are fire;
    Doubt that the sun doth move;
    Doubt truth to be a liar;
    But never doubt I love.
'O dear Ophelia, I am ill at these numbers. I have not   120
art to reckon my groans, but that I love thee best, O most
best, believe it. Adieu.
'Thine evermore, most dear lady,
    whilst this machine is to him, HAMLET.'
This in obedience hath my daughter shown me,   125

98 *figure* figure in rhetoric 105 *Perpend* ponder 118 *Doubt* suspect
120 *numbers* verses 124 *machine* body *to* attached to

And more above hath his solicitings,
As they fell out by time, by means, and place,
All given to mine ear.

King.   But how hath she
Received his love?

Polonius.   What do you think of me?

130 *King.* As of a man faithful and honorable.

Polonius. I would fain prove so. But what might you think,
When I had seen this hot love on the wing
(As I perceived it, I must tell you that,
Before my daughter told me), what might you,

135 Or my dear majesty your queen here, think,
If I had played the desk or table book,
Or given my heart a winking, mute and dumb,
Or looked upon this love with idle sight?
What might you think? No, I went round to work

140 And my young mistress thus I did bespeak:
'Lord Hamlet is a prince, out of thy star.
This must not be.' And then I prescripts gave her,
That she should lock herself from his resort,
Admit no messengers, receive no tokens.

145 Which done, she took the fruits of my advice,
And he, repellèd, a short tale to make,
Fell into a sadness, then into a fast,
Thence to a watch, thence into a weakness,
Thence to a lightness, and, by this declension,

150 Into the madness wherein now he raves,
And all we mourn for.

King.   Do you think 'tis this?

---

126 *above* besides   136 *desk or table book* i. e. silent receiver   137 *winking* closing of the eyes   139 *round* roundly, plainly   141 *star* condition determined by stellar influence   142 *prescripts* instructions   148 *watch* sleepless state   149 *lightness* lightheadedness

Queen. It may be, very like.

Polonius. Hath there been such a time — I would fain know
    that —
  That I have positively said 'Tis so,'
  When it proved otherwise?

King.   Not that I know.   155

Polonius. [pointing to his head and shoulder] Take this from
    this, if this be otherwise.
  If circumstances lead me, I will find
  Where truth is hid, though it were hid indeed
  Within the center.

King.   How may we try it further?

Polonius. You know sometimes he walks four hours together 160
  Here in the lobby.

Queen.   So he does indeed.

Polonius. At such a time I'll loose my daughter to him.
  Be you and I behind an arras then.
  Mark the encounter. If he love her not,
  And be not from his reason fallen thereon,   165
  Let me be no assistant for a state
  But keep a farm and carters.

King.   We will try it.

Enter Hamlet [reading on a book].

Queen. But look where sadly the poor wretch comes read-
    ing.

Polonius. Away, I do beseech you both, away.

                   Exit King and Queen [with Attendants].

  I'll board him presently. O, give me leave.   170

159 *center* center of the earth and also of the Ptolemaic universe 163 *arras*
hanging tapestry 165 *thereon* on that account 170 *board* accost *presently*
at once

How does my good Lord Hamlet?

Hamlet. Well, God-a-mercy.

Polonius. Do you know me, my lord?

Hamlet. Excellent well. You are a fishmonger.

175 *Polonius.* Not I, my lord.

Hamlet. Then I would you were so honest a man.

Polonius. Honest, my lord?

Hamlet. Ay, sir. To be honest, as this world goes, is to be
one man picked out of ten thousand.

180 *Polonius.* That's very true, my lord.

Hamlet. For if the sun breed maggots in a dead dog, being
a good kissing carrion — Have you a daughter?

Polonius. I have, my lord.

Hamlet. Let her not walk i' th' sun. Conception is a blessing,
185 but as your daughter may conceive, friend, look to't.

Polonius. [aside] How say you by that? Still harping on my
daughter. Yet he knew me not at first. 'A said I was a fishmonger. 'A is far gone, far gone. And truly in my youth I
suffered much extremity for love, very near this. I'll speak
190 to him again. — What do you read, my lord?

Hamlet. Words, words, words.

Polonius. What is the matter, my lord?

Hamlet. Between who?

Polonius. I mean the matter that you read, my lord.

195 *Hamlet.* Slanders, sir, for the satirical rogue says here that
old men have grey beards, that their faces are wrinkled,
their eyes purging thick amber and plum-tree gum, and
that they have a plentiful lack of wit, together with most
weak hams. All which, sir, though I most powerfully and

172 *God-a-mercy* thank you (literally, 'God have mercy!')   174 *fishmonger*
seller of harlots, procurer (a cant term used here with a glance at the
fishing Polonius is doing when he offers Ophelia as bait)   182 *good kissing
carrion* good bit of flesh for kissing   193 *Between who* matter for a quarrel
between what persons (Hamlet's willful misunderstanding)

potently believe, yet I hold it not honesty to have it thus 200
set down, for you yourself, sir, should be old as I am if,
like a crab, you could go backward.

Polonius. [aside] Though this be madness, yet there is method
in't. — Will you walk out of the air, my lord?

Hamlet. Into my grave? 205

Polonius. Indeed, that's out of the air. [aside] How pregnant
sometimes his replies are! a happiness that often madness
hits on, which reason and sanity could not so prosper-
ously be delivered of. I will leave him and suddenly contrive the means of meeting between him and my daugh- 210
ter. — My honorable lord, I will most humbly take my
leave of you.

Hamlet. You cannot, sir, take from me anything that I will
more willingly part withal — except my life, except my
life, except my life. 215

Enter Guildenstern and Rosencrantz.

Polonius. Fare you well, my lord.

Hamlet. These tedious old fools!

Polonius. You go to seek the Lord Hamlet. There he is.

Rosencrantz. [to Polonius] God save you, sir! [Exit Polonius.]

Guildenstern. My honored lord! 220

Rosencrantz. My most dear lord!

Hamlet. My excellent good friends! How dost thou, Guildenstern? Ah, Rosencrantz! Good lads, how do ye both?

Rosencrantz. As the indifferent children of the earth.

Guildenstern. Happy in that we are not over-happy. 225
On Fortune's cap we are not the very button.

Hamlet. Nor the soles of her shoe?

206 *pregnant* full of meaning   207 *happiness* aptness of expression
214 *withal* with   224 *indifferent* average

Rosencrantz. Neither, my lord.

Hamlet. Then you live about her waist, or in the middle of
230   her favors?

Guildenstern. Faith, her privates we.

Hamlet. In the secret parts of Fortune? O, most true! she is
  a strumpet. What news?

Rosencrantz. None, my lord, but that the world's grown
235   honest.

Hamlet. Then is doomsday near. But your news is not true.
  [Let me question more in particular. What have you, my
  good friends, deserved at the hands of Fortune that she
  sends you to prison hither?

240 *Guildenstern.* Prison, my lord?

Hamlet. Denmark's a prison.

Rosencrantz. Then is the world one.

Hamlet. A goodly one; in which there are many confines,
  wards, and dungeons, Denmark being one o' th' worst.

245 *Rosencrantz.* We think not so, my lord.

Hamlet. Why, then 'tis none to you, for there is nothing
  either good or bad but thinking makes it so. To me it is a
  prison.

Rosencrantz. Why, then your ambition makes it one. 'Tis
250   too narrow for your mind.

Hamlet. O God, I could be bounded in a nutshell and count
  myself a king of infinite space, were it not that I have bad
  dreams.

Guildenstern. Which dreams indeed are ambition, for the
255   very substance of the ambitious is merely the shadow of a
  dream.

Hamlet. A dream itself is but a shadow.

231 *privates* ordinary men in private, not public, life (with obvious play
upon the sexual term 'private parts')   243 *confines* places of imprisonment
244 *wards* cells

Rosencrantz. Truly, and I hold ambition of so airy and light
   a quality that it is but a shadow's shadow.

Hamlet. Then are our beggars bodies, and our monarchs   260
   and outstretched heroes the beggars' shadows. Shall we to
   th' court? for, by my fay, I cannot reason.

Both. We'll wait upon you.

Hamlet. No such matter. I will not sort you with the rest of
   my servants, for, to speak to you like an honest man, I am   265
   most dreadfully attended.] But in the beaten way of
   friendship, what make you at Elsinore?

Rosencrantz. To visit you, my lord; no other occasion.

Hamlet. Beggar that I am, I am even poor in thanks, but I
   thank you; and sure, dear friends, my thanks are too dear   270
   a halfpenny. Were you not sent for? Is it your own in-
   clining? Is it a free visitation? Come, come, deal justly
   with me. Come, come. Nay, speak.

Guildenstern. What should we say, my lord?

Hamlet. Why, anything – but to th' purpose. You were   275
   sent for, and there is a kind of confession in your looks,
   which your modesties have not craft enough to color.
   I know the good king and queen have sent for you.

Rosencrantz. To what end, my lord?

Hamlet. That you must teach me. But let me conjure you   280
   by the rights of our fellowship, by the consonancy of our
   youth, by the obligation of our ever-preserved love, and
   by what more dear a better proposer can charge you
   withal, be even and direct with me whether you were
   sent for or no.   285

260 *bodies* solid substances, not shadows (because beggars lack ambition)
261 *outstretched* elongated as shadows (with a corollary implication of far
reaching with respect to the ambitions that make both heroes and monarchs into shadows) 262 *fay* faith   263 *wait upon* attend   267 *make* do
271 *a halfpenny* at a halfpenny   281 *consonancy* accord (in sameness of age)
283 *proposer* propounder   284 *withal* with   *even* straight

75

Rosencrantz. *[aside to Guildenstern]* What say you?

Hamlet. *[aside]* Nay then, I have an eye of you. — If you love me, hold not off.

Guildenstern. My lord, we were sent for.

290 *Hamlet.* I will tell you why. So shall my anticipation prevent your discovery, and your secrecy to the king and queen moult no feather. I have of late — but wherefore I know not — lost all my mirth, forgone all custom of exercises; and indeed, it goes so heavily with my disposition
295 that this goodly frame the earth seems to me a sterile promontory; this most excellent canopy, the air, look you, this brave o'erhanging firmament, this majestical roof fretted with golden fire — why, it appeareth nothing to me but a foul and pestilent congregation of vapors.
300 What a piece of work is a man, how noble in reason, how infinite in faculties, in form and moving how express and admirable, in action how like an angel, in apprehension how like a god: the beauty of the world, the paragon of animals! And yet to me what is this quintessence of
305 dust? Man delights not me — nor woman neither, though by your smiling you seem to say so.

Rosencrantz. My lord, there was no such stuff in my thoughts.

Hamlet. Why did ye laugh then, when I said 'Man delights not me'?

310 *Rosencrantz.* To think, my lord, if you delight not in man, what lenten entertainment the players shall receive from you. We coted them on the way, and hither are they coming to offer you service.

Hamlet. He that plays the king shall be welcome — his maj-

290-91 *prevent* forestall   291 *discovery* disclosure   292 *moult no feather* be left whole   297 *firmament* sky   298 *fretted* decorated with fretwork 301-2 *express* well framed   304 *quintessence* fifth or last and finest essence (an alchemical term)   311 *lenten* scanty   312 *coted* overtook

esty shall have tribute of me —, the adventurous knight 315
shall use his foil and target, the lover shall not sigh gratis,
the humorous man shall end his part in peace, the clown
shall make those laugh whose lungs are tickle o' th' sere,
and the lady shall say her mind freely, or the blank verse
shall halt for't. What players are they? 320

Rosencrantz. Even those you were wont to take such delight in, the tragedians of the city.

Hamlet. How chances it they travel? Their residence, both
in reputation and profit, was better both ways.

Rosencrantz. I think their inhibition comes by the means of 325
the late innovation.

Hamlet. Do they hold the same estimation they did when I
was in the city? Are they so followed?

Rosencrantz. No indeed, are they not.

[*Hamlet.* How comes it? Do they grow rusty? 330

Rosencrantz. Nay, their endeavor keeps in the wonted pace,
but there is, sir, an eyrie of children, little eyases, that cry
out on the top of question and are most tyrannically
clapped for't. These are now the fashion, and so berattle
the common stages (so they call them) that many wearing 335
rapiers are afraid of goosequills and dare scarce come
thither.

316 *foil and target* sword and shield 317 *humorous man* eccentric character
dominated by one of the humors 318 *tickle o' th' sere* hair-triggered for
the discharge of laughter (*sere* = part of a gunlock) 320 *halt* go lame
323 *residence* residing at the capital 325 *inhibition* impediment to acting
in residence (formal prohibition?) 326 *innovation* new fashion of having
companies of boy actors play on the 'private' stage (?); political upheaval
(?) 332 *eyrie* nest *eyases* nestling hawks 333 *on the top of question* above
others on matter of dispute 334 *berattle* berate 335 *common stages* 'public'
theatres of the 'common' players, who were organized in companies
mainly composed of adult actors (allusion being made to the 'War of the
Theatres' in Shakespeare's London) 336 *goosequills* pens (of satirists who
made out that the London public stage showed low taste)

Hamlet. What, are they children? Who maintains 'em? How are they escoted? Will they pursue the quality no
340   longer than they can sing? Will they not say afterwards, if they should grow themselves to common players (as it is most like, if their means are no better), their writers do them wrong to make them exclaim against their own succession?

345   *Rosencrantz.* Faith, there has been much to do on both sides, and the nation holds it no sin to tarre them to controversy. There was, for a while, no money bid for argument unless the poet and the player went to cuffs in the question.

Hamlet. Is't possible?

350   *Guildenstern.* O, there has been much throwing about of brains.

Hamlet. Do the boys carry it away?

Rosencrantz. Ay, that they do, my lord – Hercules and his load too.]

355   *Hamlet.* It is not very strange, for my uncle is King of Denmark, and those that would make mows at him while my father lived give twenty, forty, fifty, a hundred ducats apiece for his picture in little. 'Sblood, there is something in this more than natural, if philosophy could find it out.
                                                              A flourish.

360   *Guildenstern.* There are the players.

Hamlet. Gentlemen, you are welcome to Elsinore. Your hands, come then. Th' appurtenance of welcome is fashion and ceremony. Let me comply with you in this garb, lest my extent to the players (which I tell you must show
365   fairly outwards) should more appear like entertainment

339 *escoted* supported   *quality* profession of acting   340 *sing* i.e. with unchanged voices   346 *tarre* incite   347 *argument* matter of a play   354 *load* i.e. the whole world (with a topical reference to the sign of the Globe Theatre, a representation of Hercules bearing the world on his shoulders)   356 *mows* grimaces   358 *'Sblood* by God's blood   363 *garb* fashion   364 *extent* showing of welcome

than yours. You are welcome. But my uncle-father and
aunt-mother are deceived.

Guildenstern. In what, my dear lord?

Hamlet. I am but mad north-north-west. When the wind is
southerly I know a hawk from a handsaw.   370

Enter Polonius.

Polonius. Well be with you, gentlemen.

Hamlet. Hark you, Guildenstern — and you too — at each
ear a hearer. That great baby you see there is not yet out
of his swaddling clouts.

Rosencrantz. Happily he is the second time come to them,   375
for they say an old man is twice a child.

Hamlet. I will prophesy he comes to tell me of the players.
Mark it. — You say right, sir; a Monday morning, 'twas
then indeed.

Polonius. My lord, I have news to tell you.   380

Hamlet. My lord, I have news to tell you. When Roscius
was an actor in Rome —

Polonius. The actors are come hither, my lord.

Hamlet. Buzz, buzz.

Polonius. Upon my honor —   385

Hamlet. Then came each actor on his ass —

Polonius. The best actors in the world, either for tragedy,
comedy, history, pastoral, pastoral-comical, historical-
pastoral, tragical-historical, tragical-comical-historical-
pastoral; scene individable, or poem unlimited. Seneca   390

370 *hawk* mattock or pickaxe (also called 'hack'; here used apparently
with a play on *hawk* = a bird) *handsaw* carpenter's tool (apparently with
a play on some corrupt form of *hernshaw* = heron, a bird often hunted
with the hawk) 374 *clouts* clothes 375 *Happily* haply, perhaps 381 *Roscius* the greatest of Roman comic actors 390 *scene individable* drama observing the unities *poem unlimited* drama not observing the unities *Seneca*
Roman writer of tragedies

cannot be too heavy, nor Plautus too light. For the law
of writ and the liberty, these are the only men.

Hamlet. O Jephthah, judge of Israel, what a treasure hadst
thou!

395 *Polonius.* What treasure had he, my lord?

Hamlet. Why,

> 'One fair daughter, and no more,
>   The which he lovèd passing well.'

Polonius. [aside] Still on my daughter.

400 *Hamlet.* Am I not i' th' right, old Jephthah?

Polonius. If you call me Jephthah, my lord, I have a daughter that I love passing well.

Hamlet. Nay, that follows not.

Polonius. What follows then, my lord?

405 *Hamlet.* Why,

> 'As by lot, God wot,'

and then, you know,

> 'It came to pass, as most like it was.'

The first row of the pious chanson will show you more,
410 for look where my abridgment comes.

Enter the Players.

You are welcome, masters, welcome, all. — I am glad to
see thee well. — Welcome, good friends. — O, old friend,
why, thy face is valanced since I saw thee last. Com'st
thou to beard me in Denmark? — What, my young lady
415 and mistress? By'r Lady, your ladyship is nearer to heaven

---

391 *Plautus* Roman writer of comedies   391–92 *law of writ* orthodoxy determined by critical rules of the drama   392 *liberty* freedom from such orthodoxy   393 *Jephthah* the compelled sacrificer of a dearly beloved
daughter (Judges 11)   398 *passing* surpassingly (verses quoted being from
a ballad on Jephthah)   409 *row* stanza   *chanson* song   410 *my abridgment*
that which shortens my talk   413 *valanced* fringed (with a beard)
414 *young lady* boy who plays women's parts

80

than when I saw you last by the altitude of a chopine.
Pray God your voice, like a piece of uncurrent gold, be
not cracked within the ring. — Masters, you are all welcome. We'll e'en to't like French falconers, fly at anything
we see. We'll have a speech straight. Come, give us a   420
taste of your quality. Come, a passionate speech.

Player. What speech, my good lord?

Hamlet. I heard thee speak me a speech once, but it was
never acted, or if it was, not above once, for the play, I
remember, pleased not the million; 'twas caviary to the   425
general, but it was (as I received it, and others, whose
judgments in such matters cried in the top of mine) an
excellent play, well digested in the scenes, set down with
as much modesty as cunning. I remember one said there
were no sallets in the lines to make the matter savory,   430
nor no matter in the phrase that might indict the author
of affectation, but called it an honest method, as wholesome as sweet, and by very much more handsome than
fine. One speech in't I chiefly loved. 'Twas Aeneas' tale to
Dido, and thereabout of it especially where he speaks of   435
Priam's slaughter. If it live in your memory, begin at this
line — let me see, let me see:

'The rugged Pyrrhus, like th' Hyrcanian beast —'
'Tis not so; it begins with Pyrrhus:

'The rugged Pyrrhus, he whose sable arms,   440
Black as his purpose, did the night resemble
When he lay couchèd in the ominous horse,

---

416 *chopine* women's thick-soled shoe 417 *uncurrent* not legal tender
418 *within the ring* from the edge through the line circling the design on the
coin (with a play on *ring* = a sound) 425 *caviary* caviare 426 *general*
multitude 427 *in the top of* more authoritatively than 430 *sallets* salads,
highly seasoned passages 436 *Priam's slaughter* i.e. at the fall of Troy
(Aeneid ii, 506 ff.) 438 *Hyrcanian beast* tiger 440 *sable* black 442 *ominous* fateful *horse* the wooden horse by which the Greeks gained entrance
to Troy

Hath now this dread and black complexion smeared
With heraldry more dismal. Head to foot
445 Now is he total gules, horridly tricked
With blood of fathers, mothers, daughters, sons
Baked and impasted with the parching streets,
That lend a tyrannous and a damnèd light
To their lord's murther. Roasted in wrath and fire,
450 And thus o'ersizèd with coagulate gore,
With eyes like carbuncles, the hellish Pyrrhus
Old grandsire Priam seeks.'
So, proceed you.

Polonius. Fore God, my lord, well spoken, with good ac-
455 cent and good discretion.

Player.   'Anon he finds him,
Striking too short at Greeks. His antique sword,
Rebellious to his arm, lies where it falls,
Repugnant to command. Unequal matched,
460 Pyrrhus at Priam drives, in rage strikes wide,
But with the whiff and wind of his fell sword
Th' unnervèd father falls. Then senseless Ilium,
Seeming to feel this blow, with flaming top
Stoops to his base, and with a hideous crash
465 Takes prisoner Pyrrhus' ear. For lo! his sword,
Which was declining on the milky head
Of reverend Priam, seemed i' th' air to stick
So as a painted tyrant Pyrrhus stood,
And like a neutral to his will and matter
470 Did nothing.

444 *dismal* ill-omened 445 *gules* red (heraldic term) *tricked* decorated in
color (heraldic term) 447 *parching* i.e. because Troy was burning 450 *oer-
sizèd* covered as with size, a glutinous material used for filling pores of
plaster, etc. *coagulate* clotted 461 *fell* cruel 462 *senseless* without feeling 464 *his* its 468 *painted* pictured 469 *will and matter* purpose and its
realization (between which he stands motionless)

82

But as we often see, against some storm,
A silence in the heavens, the rack stand still,
The bold winds speechless, and the orb below
As hush as death, anon the dreadful thunder
Doth rend the region, so after Pyrrhus' pause,   475
Arousèd vengeance sets him new awork,
And never did the Cyclops' hammers fall
On Mars's armor, forged for proof eterne,
With less remorse than Pyrrhus' bleeding sword
Now falls on Priam.   480
Out, out, thou strumpet Fortune! All you gods,
In general synod take away her power,
Break all the spokes and fellies from her wheel,
And bowl the round nave down the hill of heaven,
As low as to the fiends.'   485

Polonius. This is too long.

Hamlet. It shall to the barber's, with your beard. — Prithee
say on. He's for a jig or a tale of bawdry, or he sleeps. Say
on; come to Hecuba.

Player. 'But who (ah woe!) had seen the mobled queen —'   490

Hamlet. 'The mobled queen'?

Polonius. That's good. 'Mobled queen' is good.

Player. 'Run barefoot up and down, threat'ning the flames
        With bisson rheum; a clout upon that head
        Where late the diadem stood, and for a robe,   495
        About her lank and all o'erteemèd loins,
        A blanket in the alarm of fear caught up —
        Who this had seen, with tongue in venom steeped

---

471 *against* just before   472 *rack* clouds   475 *region* sky   477 *Cyclops* giant
workmen who made armor in the smithy of Vulcan   478 *proof eterne* eternal protection   483 *fellies* segments of the rim   484 *nave* hub   488 *jig*
short comic piece with singing and dancing often presented after a play
490 *mobled* muffled   494 *bisson rheum* blinding tears   *clout* cloth   496 *o'er-
teemèd* overproductive of children

'Gainst Fortune's state would treason have pronounced.
500   But if the gods themselves did see her then,
When she saw Pyrrhus make malicious sport
In mincing with his sword her husband's limbs,
The instant burst of clamor that she made
(Unless things mortal move them not at all)
505   Would have made milch the burning eyes of heaven
And passion in the gods.'

Polonius. Look, whe'r he has not turned his color, and has
tears in's eyes. Prithee no more.

Hamlet. 'Tis well. I'll have thee speak out the rest of this
510   soon. — Good my lord, will you see the players well bestowed? Do you hear? Let them be well used, for they
are the abstract and brief chronicles of the time. After your
death you were better have a bad epitaph than their ill report while you live.

515 *Polonius.* My lord, I will use them according to their desert.

Hamlet. God's bodkin, man, much better! Use every man
after his desert, and who shall scape whipping? Use them
after your own honor and dignity. The less they deserve,
the more merit is in your bounty. Take them in.

520 *Polonius.* Come, sirs.

Hamlet. Follow him, friends. We'll hear a play to-morrow.
[aside to Player] Dost thou hear me, old friend? Can you
play 'The Murther of Gonzago'?

Player. Ay, my lord.

525 *Hamlet.* We'll ha't to-morrow night. You could for a need
study a speech of some dozen or sixteen lines which I
would set down and insert in't, could you not?

Player. Ay, my lord.

---

499 *state* government of worldly events   505 *milch* tearful (milk-giving)
eyes i.e. stars   507 *whe'r* whether   510–11 *bestowed* lodged   516 *God's bodkin* by God's little body

Hamlet. Very well. Follow that lord, and look you mock
   him not. — My good friends, I'll leave you till night. You   530
   are welcome to Elsinore.   *Exeunt Polonius and Players.*
Rosencrantz. Good my lord.
                              Exeunt [Rosencrantz and Guildenstern].
Hamlet. Ay, so, God bye to you. — Now I am alone.
   O, what a rogue and peasant slave am I!
   Is it not monstrous that this player here,   535
   But in a fiction, in a dream of passion,
   Could force his soul so to his own conceit
   That from her working all his visage wanned,
   Tears in his eyes, distraction in his aspect,
   A broken voice, and his whole function suiting   540
   With forms to his conceit? And all for nothing,
   For Hecuba!
   What's Hecuba to him, or he to Hecuba,
   That he should weep for her? What would he do
   Had he the motive and the cue for passion   545
   That I have? He would drown the stage with tears
   And cleave the general ear with horrid speech,
   Make mad the guilty and appal the free,
   Confound the ignorant, and amaze indeed
   The very faculties of eyes and ears.   550
   Yet I,
   A dull and muddy-mettled rascal, peak
   Like John-a-dreams, unpregnant of my cause,
   And can say nothing. No, not for a king,
   Upon whose property and most dear life   555
   A damned defeat was made. Am I a coward?
   Who calls me villain? breaks my pate across?

537 *conceit* conception, idea 540 *function* action of bodily powers 552 *mud-dy-mettled* dull-spirited *peak* mope 553 *John-a-dreams* a sleepy dawdler *unpregnant* barren of realization

Plucks off my beard and blows it in my face?
Tweaks me by the nose? gives me the lie i' th' throat
560 As deep as to the lungs? Who does me this?
Ha, 'swounds, I should take it, for it cannot be
But I am pigeon-livered and lack gall
To make oppression bitter, or ere this
I should ha' fatted all the region kites
565 With this slave's offal. Bloody, bawdy villain!
Remorseless, treacherous, lecherous, kindless villain!
O, vengeance!
Why, what an ass am I! This is most brave,
That I, the son of a dear father murthered,
570 Prompted to my revenge by heaven and hell,
Must like a whore unpack my heart with words
And fall a-cursing like a very drab,
A stallion! Fie upon't, foh! About, my brains.
Hum —
575 I have heard that guilty creatures sitting at a play
Have by the very cunning of the scene
Been struck so to the soul that presently
They have proclaimed their malefactions.
For murther, though it have no tongue, will speak
580 With most miraculous organ. I'll have these players
Play something like the murther of my father
Before mine uncle. I'll observe his looks.
I'll tent him to the quick. If 'a do blench,
I know my course. The spirit that I have seen
585 May be a devil, and the devil hath power
T' assume a pleasing shape, yea, and perhaps

561 *'swounds* by God's wounds   562 *pigeon-livered* of dovelike gentleness
564 *region kites* kites of the air   565 *offal* guts   566 *kindless* unnatural
573 *stallion* prostitute (male or female)   577 *presently* immediately   583 *tent*
probe   *blench* flinch

86

Out of my weakness and my melancholy,
As he is very potent with such spirits,
Abuses me to damn me. I'll have grounds
More relative than this. The play's the thing   590
Wherein I'll catch the conscience of the king.   *Exit.*

❖

Enter King, Queen, Polonius, Ophelia, Rosencrantz,   III, i
Guildenstern, Lords.

King. And can you by no drift of conference
 Get from him why he puts on this confusion,
 Grating so harshly all his days of quiet
 With turbulent and dangerous lunacy?
Rosencrantz. He does confess he feels himself distracted,   5
 But from what cause 'a will by no means speak.
Guildenstern. Nor do we find him forward to be sounded,
 But with a crafty madness keeps aloof
 When we would bring him on to some confession
 Of his true state.
Queen.   Did he receive you well?   10
Rosencrantz. Most like a gentleman.
Guildenstern. But with much forcing of his disposition.
Rosencrantz. Niggard of question, but of our demands
 Most free in his reply.
Queen.   Did you assay him
 To any pastime?
Rosencrantz. Madam, it so fell out that certain players
 We o'erraught on the way. Of these we told him,

589 *Abuses* deludes   590 *relative* pertinent   III, i, 1 *drift of conference*
direction of conversation   14 *assay* try to win   17 *o'erraught* overtook

And there did seem in him a kind of joy
To hear of it. They are here about the court,
20 And, as I think, they have already order
This night to play before him.

Polonius.   'Tis most true,
And he beseeched me to entreat your majesties
To hear and see the matter.

King. With all my heart, and it doth much content me
25 To hear him so inclined.
Good gentlemen, give him a further edge
And drive his purpose into these delights.

Rosencrantz. We shall, my lord.

                       Exeunt Rosencrantz and Guildenstern.

King.   Sweet Gertrude, leave us too,
For we have closely sent for Hamlet hither,
30 That he, as 'twere by accident, may here
Affront Ophelia.
Her father and myself (lawful espials)
Will so bestow ourselves that, seeing unseen,
We may of their encounter frankly judge
35 And gather by him, as he is behaved,
If 't be th' affliction of his love or no
That thus he suffers for.

Queen.   I shall obey you. —
And for your part, Ophelia, I do wish
That your good beauties be the happy cause
40 Of Hamlet's wildness. So shall I hope your virtues
Will bring him to his wonted way again,
To both your honors.

Ophelia.   Madam, I wish it may. *[Exit Queen.]*

Polonius. Ophelia, walk you here. — Gracious, so please you,

26 *edge* keenness of desire   29 *closely* privately   31 *Affront* come face to
face with   32 *espials* spies

We will bestow ourselves. — *[to Ophelia]* Read on this
  book,
That show of such an exercise may color   45
Your loneliness. We are oft to blame in this,
'Tis too much proved, that with devotion's visage
And pious action we do sugar o'er
The devil himself.
King.   *[aside]* O, 'tis too true.
How smart a lash that speech doth give my conscience!   50
The harlot's cheek, beautied with plast'ring art,
Is not more ugly to the thing that helps it
Than is my deed to my most painted word.
O heavy burthen!
Polonius. I hear him coming. Let's withdraw, my lord.   55
                         [Exeunt King and Polonius.]

Enter Hamlet.

Hamlet. To be, or not to be — that is the question:
Whether 'tis nobler in the mind to suffer
The slings and arrows of outrageous fortune
Or to take arms against a sea of troubles
And by opposing end them. To die, to sleep —   60
No more — and by a sleep to say we end
The heartache, and the thousand natural shocks
That flesh is heir to. 'Tis a consummation
Devoutly to be wished. To die, to sleep —
To sleep — perchance to dream: ay, there's the rub,   65
For in that sleep of death what dreams may come
When we have shuffled off this mortal coil,

45 *exercise* religious exercise (the book being obviously one of devotion)
color give an appearance of naturalness to   52 *to* compared to   65 *rub*
obstacle (literally, obstruction encountered by a bowler's ball)   67 *shuffled
off* cast off as an encumbrance   *coil* to-do, turmoil

       Must give us pause. There's the respect
       That makes calamity of so long life.
70   For who would bear the whips and scorns of time,
       Th' oppressor's wrong, the proud man's contumely
       The pangs of despised love, the law's delay,
       The insolence of office, and the spurns
       That patient merit of th' unworthy takes,
75   When he himself might his quietus make
       With a bare bodkin? Who would fardels bear,
       To grunt and sweat under a weary life,
       But that the dread of something after death,
       The undiscovered country, from whose bourn
80   No traveller returns, puzzles the will,
       And makes us rather bear those ills we have
       Than fly to others that we know not of?
       Thus conscience does make cowards of us all,
       And thus the native hue of resolution
85   Is sicklied o'er with the pale cast of thought,
       And enterprises of great pitch and moment
       With this regard their currents turn awry
       And lose the name of action. — Soft you now,
       The fair Ophelia! — Nymph, in thy orisons
       Be all my sins remembered.
90 *Ophelia.*   Good my lord,
       How does your honor for this many a day?
   Hamlet. I humbly thank you, well, well, well.
   Ophelia. My lord, I have remembrances of yours
       That I have longèd long to re-deliver.
       I pray you, now receive them.

68 *respect* consideration 69 *of so long life* so long-lived 75 *quietus* settlement (literally, release from debt) 76 *bodkin* dagger *fardels* burdens 79 *bourn* confine, region 86 *pitch* height (of a soaring falcon's flight) 87 *regard* consideration 89 *orisons* prayers (because of the book of devotion she reads)

Hamlet.   No, not I,   95
    I never gave you aught.

Ophelia. My honored lord, you know right well you did,
    And with them words of so sweet breath composed
    As made the things more rich. Their perfume lost,
    Take these again, for to the noble mind   100
    Rich gifts wax poor when givers prove unkind.
    There, my lord.

Hamlet. Ha, ha! Are you honest?

Ophelia. My lord?

Hamlet. Are you fair?   105

Ophelia. What means your lordship?

Hamlet. That if you be honest and fair, your honesty should
    admit no discourse to your beauty.

Ophelia. Could beauty, my lord, have better commerce
    than with honesty?   110

Hamlet. Ay, truly; for the power of beauty will sooner
    transform honesty from what it is to a bawd than the
    force of honesty can translate beauty into his likeness.
    This was sometime a paradox, but now the time gives it
    proof. I did love you once.   115

Ophelia. Indeed, my lord, you made me believe so.

Hamlet. You should not have believed me, for virtue cannot
    so inoculate our old stock but we shall relish of it. I loved
    you not.

Ophelia. I was the more deceived.   120

Hamlet. Get thee to a nunnery. Why wouldst thou be a
    breeder of sinners? I am myself indifferent honest, but yet
    I could accuse me of such things that it were better my
    mother had not borne me: I am very proud, revengeful,

---

103 *honest* chaste   109 *commerce* intercourse   114 *paradox* idea contrary to common opinion   118 *inoculate* graft   *relish* have a flavor (because of original sin)   122 *indifferent honest* moderately respectable

125   ambitious, with more offenses at my beck than I have
thoughts to put them in, imagination to give them
shape, or time to act them in. What should such fellows
as I do crawling between earth and heaven? We are
arrant knaves all; believe none of us. Go thy ways to a
130   nunnery. Where's your father?

Ophelia. At home, my lord.

Hamlet. Let the doors be shut upon him, that he may play
the fool nowhere but in's own house. Farewell.

Ophelia. O, help him, you sweet heavens!

135 *Hamlet.* If thou dost marry, I'll give thee this plague for thy
dowry: be thou as chaste as ice, as pure as snow, thou
shalt not escape calumny. Get thee to a nunnery. Go, farewell. Or if thou wilt needs marry, marry a fool, for wise
men know well enough what monsters you make of them.
140   To a nunnery, go, and quickly too. Farewell.

Ophelia. O heavenly powers, restore him!

Hamlet. I have heard of your paintings too, well enough.
God hath given you one face, and you make yourselves
another. You jig, you amble, and you lisp; you nickname
145   God's creatures and make your wantonness your ignorance. Go to, I'll no more on't; it hath made me mad.
I say we will have no more marriage. Those that are
married already – all but one – shall live. The rest shall
keep as they are. To a nunnery, go.   *Exit.*

150 *Ophelia.* O, what a noble mind is here o'erthrown!
The courtier's, soldier's, scholar's, eye, tongue, sword,
Th' expectancy and rose of the fair state,
The glass of fashion and the mould of form,

139 *monsters* i.e. men wearing horns given by unfaithful wives, cuckolds
145 *wantonness* affectation   145–46 *your ignorance* a matter for which you
offer the excuse that you don't know any better   152 *expectancy and rose*
fair hope   153 *glass* mirror

Th' observed of all observers, quite, quite down!
And I, of ladies most deject and wretched, 155
That sucked the honey of his music vows,
Now see that noble and most sovereign reason
Like sweet bells jangled, out of time and harsh,
That unmatched form and feature of blown youth
Blasted with ecstasy. O, woe is me 160
T' have seen what I have seen, see what I see!

Enter King and Polonius.

King. Love? his affections do not that way tend,
Nor what he spake, though it lacked form a little,
Was not like madness. There's something in his soul
O'er which his melancholy sits on brood, 165
And I do doubt the hatch and the disclose
Will be some danger; which for to prevent,
I have in quick determination
Thus set it down: he shall with speed to England
For the demand of our neglected tribute. 170
Haply the seas, and countries different,
With variable objects, shall expel
This something-settled matter in his heart,
Whereon his brains still beating puts him thus
From fashion of himself. What think you on't? 175
Polonius. It shall do well. But yet do I believe
The origin and commencement of his grief
Sprung from neglected love. — How now, Ophelia?
You need not tell us what Lord Hamlet said.
We heard it all. — My lord, do as you please, 180
But if you hold it fit, after the play

160 *ecstasy* madness 162 *affections* emotions 166 *doubt* fear 173 *something-settled* somewhat settled

93

Let his queen mother all alone entreat him
To show his grief. Let her be round with him,
And I'll be placed, so please you, in the ear
185 Of all their conference. If she find him not,
To England send him, or confine him where
Your wisdom best shall think.

King.   It shall be so.
Madness in great ones must not unwatched go. *Exeunt.*

III, ii   *Enter Hamlet and three of the Players.*

Hamlet. Speak the speech, I pray you, as I pronounced it to
you, trippingly on the tongue. But if you mouth it, as
many of our players do, I had as lief the town crier spoke
my lines. Nor do not saw the air too much with your
5 hand, thus, but use all gently, for in the very torrent,
tempest, and (as I may say) whirlwind of your passion,
you must acquire and beget a temperance that may give it
smoothness. O, it offends me to the soul to hear a robustious periwig-pated fellow tear a passion to tatters, to very
10 rags, to split the ears of the groundlings, who for the most
part are capable of nothing but inexplicable dumb shows
and noise. I would have such a fellow whipped for o'er-
doing Termagant. It out-herods Herod. Pray you avoid it.
Player. I warrant your honor.

183 *round* plain-spoken   III, ii, 2 *trippingly* easily   8–9 *robustious* boister-
ous   9 *periwig-pated* wig-wearing (after the custom of actors)   10 *groundlings* spectators who paid least and stood on the ground in the pit or yard
of the theatre   11 *dumb shows* brief actions without words, forecasting dramatic matter to follow (the play presented later in this scene giving an
old-fashioned example)   13 *Termagant* a Saracen 'god' in medieval romance
and drama   *Herod* the raging tyrant of old Biblical plays

Hamlet. Be not too tame neither, but let your own dis-   15
cretion be your tutor. Suit the action to the word, the
word to the action, with this special observance, that you
o'erstep not the modesty of nature. For anything so overdone is from the purpose of playing, whose end, both at
the first and now, was and is, to hold, as 'twere, the mirror   20
up to nature, to show virtue her own feature, scorn her
own image, and the very age and body of the time his
form and pressure. Now this overdone, or come tardy off,
though it make the unskillful laugh, cannot but make the
judicious grieve, the censure of the which one must in   25
your allowance o'erweigh a whole theatre of others.
O, there be players that I have seen play, and heard others
praise, and that highly (not to speak it profanely), that
neither having th' accent of Christians, nor the gait of
Christian, pagan, nor man, have so strutted and bellowed   30
that I have thought some of Nature's journeymen had
made men, and not made them well, they imitated hu-
manity so abominably.

Player. I hope we have reformed that indifferently with us,
sir.   35

Hamlet. O, reform it altogether! And let those that play
your clowns speak no more than is set down for them, for
there be of them that will themselves laugh, to set on some
quantity of barren spectators to laugh too, though in the
mean time some necessary question of the play be then to   40
be considered. That's villainous and shows a most pitiful
ambition in the fool that uses it. Go make you ready.

                                        [Exeunt Players.]

19 *from* apart from   23 *pressure* impressed or printed character   *come
tardy off* brought off slowly and badly   25 *the censure of the which one*
the judgment of even one of whom   31 *journeymen* workmen not yet
masters of their trade   34 *indifferently* fairly well   38 *of them* some of them

Enter Polonius, Guildenstern, and Rosencrantz.

How now, my lord? Will the king hear this piece of
work?

45 *Polonius.* And the queen too, and that presently.
Hamlet. Bid the players make haste.   *[Exit Polonius.]*
     Will you two help to hasten them?
Rosencrantz. Ay, my lord.   *Exeunt they two.*
Hamlet. What, ho, Horatio!

Enter Horatio.

50 *Horatio.* Here, sweet lord, at your service.
Hamlet. Horatio, thou art e'en as just a man
     As e'er my conversation coped withal.
Horatio. O, my dear lord —
Hamlet.   Nay, do not think I flatter.
     For what advancement may I hope from thee,
55   That no revenue hast but thy good spirits
     To feed and clothe thee? Why should the poor be flat-
       tered?
     No, let the candied tongue lick absurd pomp,
     And crook the pregnant hinges of the knee
     Where thrift may follow fawning. Dost thou hear?
60   Since my dear soul was mistress of her choice
     And could of men distinguish her election,
     S' hath sealed thee for herself, for thou hast been
     As one in suff'ring all that suffers nothing,
     A man that Fortune's buffets and rewards
65   Hast ta'en with equal thanks; and blest are those
     Whose blood and judgment are so well commeddled

---

45 *presently* at once   52 *conversation coped withal* intercourse with men encountered   58 *pregnant* quick to move   59 *thrift* profit   62 *sealed* marked
66 *blood* passion   *commeddled* mixed together

That they are not a pipe for Fortune's finger
To sound what stop she please. Give me that man
That is not passion's slave, and I will wear him
In my heart's core, ay, in my heart of heart,   70
As I do thee. Something too much of this —
There is a play to-night before the king.
One scene of it comes near the circumstance
Which I have told thee, of my father's death.
I prithee, when thou seest that act afoot,   75
Even with the very comment of thy soul
Observe my uncle. If his occulted guilt
Do not itself unkennel in one speech,
It is a damnèd ghost that we have seen,
And my imaginations are as foul   80
As Vulcan's stithy. Give him heedful note,
For I mine eyes will rivet to his face,
And after we will both our judgments join
In censure of his seeming.
Horatio.   Well, my lord.
If 'a steal aught the whilst this play is playing,   85
And scape detecting, I will pay the theft.

*Enter Trumpets and Kettledrums, King, Queen, Polonius,
Ophelia, [Rosencrantz, Guildenstern, and other Lords
attendant].*

Hamlet. They are coming to the play. I must be idle.
Get you a place.
King. How fares our cousin Hamlet?

76 *the very . . . soul* thy deepest sagacity   77 *occulted* hidden   79 *damned
ghost* evil spirit, devil (as thought of in II, ii, 584 ff.)   81 *stithy* smithy
84 *censure of* sentence upon   87 *be idle* be foolish, act the madman   89 *cousin*
nephew

90 *Hamlet.* Excellent, i' faith, of the chameleon's dish. I eat the
   air, promise-crammed. You cannot feed capons so.

   King. I have nothing with this answer, Hamlet. These
   words are not mine.

   Hamlet. No, nor mine now. *[to Polonius]* My lord, you
95 played once i' th' university, you say?

   Polonius. That did I, my lord, and was accounted a good
   actor.

   Hamlet. What did you enact?

   Polonius. I did enact Julius Caesar. I was killed i' th' Capitol;
100 Brutus killed me.

   Hamlet. It was a brute part of him to kill so capital a calf
   there. Be the players ready?

   Rosencrantz. Ay, my lord. They stay upon your patience.

   Queen. Come hither, my dear Hamlet, sit by me.

105 *Hamlet.* No, good mother. Here's metal more attractive.

   Polonius. *[to the King]* O ho! do you mark that?

   Hamlet. Lady, shall I lie in your lap?

                              [He lies at Ophelia's feet.]

   Ophelia. No, my lord.

   Hamlet. I mean, my head upon your lap?

110 *Ophelia.* Ay, my lord.

   Hamlet. Do you think I meant country matters?

   Ophelia. I think nothing, my lord.

   Hamlet. That's a fair thought to lie between maids' legs.

   Ophelia. What is, my lord?

115 *Hamlet.* Nothing.

   Ophelia. You are merry, my lord.

   Hamlet. Who, I?

90 *chameleon's dish* i.e. air (which was believed the chameleon's food;
Hamlet willfully takes *fares* in the sense of 'feeds') 93 *not mine* not for
me as the asker of my question 103 *stay upon your patience* await your
indulgence 111 *country matters* rustic goings-on, barnyard mating (with a
play upon a sexual term)

Ophelia. Ay, my lord.

Hamlet. O God, your only jig-maker! What should a man
do but be merry? For look you how cheerfully my 120
mother looks, and my father died within's two hours.

Ophelia. Nay, 'tis twice two months, my lord.

Hamlet. So long? Nay then, let the devil wear black, for I'll
have a suit of sables. O heavens! die two months ago, and
not forgotten yet? Then there's hope a great man's mem- 125
ory may outlive his life half a year. But, by'r Lady, he
must build churches then, or else shall 'a suffer not thinking on, with the hobby-horse, whose epitaph is 'For O,
for O, the hobby-horse is forgot!'

The trumpets sound. Dumb show follows:

*Enter a King and a Queen [very lovingly], the Queen embracing
him, and he her. [She kneels; and makes show of protestation unto him.] He takes her up, and declines his head upon her neck.
He lies him down upon a bank of flowers. She, seeing him asleep,
leaves him. Anon come in another man: takes off his crown,
kisses it, pours poison in the sleeper's ears, and leaves him. The
Queen returns, finds the King dead, makes passionate action.
The poisoner, with some three or four, come in again, seem to
condole with her. The dead body is carried away. The poisoner
woos the Queen with gifts; she seems harsh awhile, but in the
end accepts love.* [*Exeunt.*]

Ophelia. What means this, my lord? 130

Hamlet. Marry, this is miching mallecho; it means mischief.

Ophelia. Belike this show imports the argument of the play.

---

119 *jig-maker* writer of jigs (see II, ii, 488) 124 *sables* black furs (lux-
urious garb, not for mourning) 128 *hobby-horse* traditional figure strapped
round the waist of a performer in May games and morris dances 131 *miching mallecho* sneaking iniquity

Enter Prologue.

Hamlet. We shall know by this fellow. The players cannot
    keep counsel; they'll tell all.

35 *Ophelia.* Will 'a tell us what this show meant?

Hamlet. Ay, or any show that you'll show him. Be not you
    ashamed to show, he'll not shame to tell you what it
    means.

Ophelia. You are naught, you are naught. I'll mark the play.

140 *Prologue.* For us and for our tragedy,
               Here stooping to your clemency,
               We beg your hearing patiently.   *[Exit.]*

Hamlet. Is this a prologue, or the posy of a ring?

Ophelia. 'Tis brief, my lord.

145 *Hamlet.* As woman's love.

Enter [two Players as] King and Queen.

King. Full thirty times hath Phoebus' cart gone round
    Neptune's salt wash and Tellus' orbèd ground,
    And thirty dozen moons with borrowed sheen
    About the world have times twelve thirties been,

150   Since love our hearts, and Hymen did our hands,
    Unite commutual in most sacred bands.

Queen. So many journeys may the sun and moon
    Make us again count o'er ere love be done!
    But woe is me, you are so sick of late,

155   So far from cheer and from your former state,
    That I distrust you. Yet, though I distrust,
    Discomfort you, my lord, it nothing must.

---

139 *naught* indecent   143 *posy* brief motto in rhyme ('poesy') **ring** finger
ring   146 *Phoebus' cart* the sun's chariot   147 *Tellus* Roman goddess of the
earth   148 *borrowed* i.e. taken from the sun   150 *Hymen* Greek god of
marriage   151 *commutual* mutually   156 *distrust you* fear for you

For women fear too much, even as they love,
And women's fear and love hold quantity,
In neither aught, or in extremity.   160
Now what my love is, proof hath made you know,
And as my love is sized, my fear is so.
Where love is great, the littlest doubts are fear;
Where little fears grow great, great love grows there.

King. Faith, I must leave thee, love, and shortly too;   165
My operant powers their functions leave to do.
And thou shalt live in this fair world behind,
Honored, beloved, and haply one as kind
For husband shalt thou —

Queen.   O, confound the rest!
Such love must needs be treason in my breast.   170
In second husband let me be accurst!
None wed the second but who killed the first.

Hamlet. [aside] That's wormwood.

Queen. The instances that second marriage move
Are base respects of thrift, but none of love.   175
A second time I kill my husband dead
When second husband kisses me in bed.

King. I do believe you think what now you speak,
But what we do determine oft we break.
Purpose is but the slave to memory,   180
Of violent birth, but poor validity,
Which now like fruit unripe sticks on the tree,
But fall unshaken when they mellow be.
Most necessary 'tis that we forget
To pay ourselves what to ourselves is debt.   185
What to ourselves in passion we propose,

159 *quantity* proportion 166 *operant powers* active bodily forces 173 *wormwood* a bitter herb 174 *instances* motives 180 *slave to* i.e. dependent upon
for life 181 *validity* strength

The passion ending, doth the purpose lose.
The violence of either grief or joy
Their own enactures with themselves destroy.
190   Where joy most revels, grief doth most lament;
Grief joys, joy grieves, on slender accident.
This world is not for aye, nor 'tis not strange
That even our loves should with our fortunes change,
For 'tis a question left us yet to prove,
195   Whether love lead fortune, or else fortune love.
The great man down, you mark his favorite flies,
The poor advanced makes friends of enemies;
And hitherto doth love on fortune tend,
For who not needs shall never lack a friend,
200   And who in want a hollow friend doth try,
Directly seasons him his enemy.
But, orderly to end where I begun,
Our wills and fates do so contrary run
That our devices still are overthrown;
205   Our thoughts are ours, their ends none of our own.
So think thou wilt no second husband wed,
But die thy thoughts when thy first lord is dead.
Queen. Nor earth to me give food, nor heaven light,
Sport and repose lock from me day and night,
210   To desperation turn my trust and hope,
An anchor's cheer in prison be my scope,
Each opposite that blanks the face of joy
Meet what I would have well, and it destroy,
Both here and hence pursue me lasting strife,
215   If, once a widow, ever I be wife!
Hamlet. If she should break it now!

189 *enactures* fulfillments   201 *seasons him* ripens him into   204 *still* always
211 *anchor's* hermit's   212 *blanks* blanches, makes pale   214 *hence* in the
next world

King. 'Tis deeply sworn. Sweet, leave me here awhile.
　My spirits grow dull, and fain I would beguile
　The tedious day with sleep.
Queen.　　　　　　　　Sleep rock thy brain, *[He sleeps.]*
　And never come mischance between us twain!　　*Exit.* 220
Hamlet. Madam, how like you this play?
Queen. The lady doth protest too much, methinks.
Hamlet. O, but she'll keep her word.
King. Have you heard the argument? Is there no offense
　in't?　　　　　　　　　　　　　　　　　　　　　　225
Hamlet. No, no, they do but jest, poison in jest; no offense
　i' th' world.
King. What do you call the play?
Hamlet. 'The Mousetrap.' Marry, how? Tropically. This
　play is the image of a murther done in Vienna. Gonzago is 230
　the duke's name; his wife, Baptista. You shall see anon.
　'Tis a knavish piece of work, but what o' that? Your
　majesty, and we that have free souls, it touches us not.
　Let the galled jade winch; our withers are unwrung.

Enter Lucianus.

This is one Lucianus, nephew to the king.　　　　　235
Ophelia. You are as good as a chorus, my lord.
Hamlet. I could interpret between you and your love, if I
　could see the puppets dallying.
Ophelia. You are keen, my lord, you are keen.
Hamlet. It would cost you a groaning to take off my edge. 240
Ophelia. Still better, and worse.
Hamlet. So you must take your husbands. — Begin, mur-

224 *argument* plot summary　229 *Tropically* in the way of a trope or figure
(with a play on 'trapically')　233 *free* guiltless　234 *galled* sore-backed　*jade*
horse　*winch* wince　*withers* shoulders　236 *chorus* one in a play who
explains the action　238 *puppets* i.e. you and your lover as in a puppet
show

therer. Leave thy damnable faces and begin. Come, the croaking raven doth bellow for revenge.

Lucianus. Thoughts black, hands apt, drugs fit, and time

245   agreeing,

Confederate season, else no creature seeing,

Thou mixture rank, of midnight weeds collected,

With Hecate's ban thrice blasted, thrice infected,

Thy natural magic and dire property

250 On wholesome life usurps immediately.

[Pours the poison in his ears.]

Hamlet. 'A poisons him i' th' garden for his estate. His name's Gonzago. The story is extant, and written in very choice Italian. You shall see anon how the murtherer gets the love of Gonzago's wife.

255 *Ophelia.* The king rises.

Hamlet. What, frighted with false fire?

Queen. How fares my lord?

Polonius. Give o'er the play.

King. Give me some light. Away!

260 *Polonius.* Lights, lights, lights!

Exeunt all but Hamlet and Horatio.

Hamlet. Why, let the strucken deer go weep,

The hart ungallèd play.

For some must watch, while some must sleep;

Thus runs the world away.

265 Would not this, sir, and a forest of feathers — if the rest of my fortunes turn Turk with me — with two Provincial roses on my razed shoes, get me a fellowship in a cry of players, sir?

246 *Confederate season* the occasion being my ally   248 *Hecate* goddess of witchcraft and black magic   *ban* curse   256 *false fire* a firing of a gun charged with powder but no shot, a blank-discharge   265 *feathers* plumes for actors' costumes   266 *turn Turk* turn renegade, like a Christian turning Mohammedan   266–67 *Provincial roses* ribbon rosettes   267 *razed* decorated with cut patterns   *cry* pack

Horatio. Half a share.

Hamlet. A whole one, I.   270
  For thou dost know, O Damon dear,
    This realm dismantled was
  Of Jove himself; and now reigns here
    A very, very — peacock.

Horatio. You might have rhymed.   275

Hamlet. O good Horatio, I'll take the ghost's word for a
  thousand pound. Didst perceive?

Horatio. Very well, my lord.

Hamlet. Upon the talk of the poisoning?

Horatio. I did very well note him.   280

Hamlet. Aha! Come, some music! Come, the recorders!
  For if the king like not the comedy,
  Why then, belike he likes it not, perdy.
  Come, some music!

Enter Rosencrantz and Guildenstern.

Guildenstern. Good my lord, vouchsafe me a word with you. 285

Hamlet. Sir, a whole history.

Guildenstern. The king, sir —

Hamlet. Ay, sir, what of him?

Guildenstern. Is in his retirement marvellous distempered.

Hamlet. With drink, sir?   290

Guildenstern. No, my lord, with choler.

Hamlet. Your wisdom should show itself more richer to
  signify this to the doctor, for for me to put him to his
  purgation would perhaps plunge him into more choler.

Guildenstern. Good my lord, put your discourse into some 295
  frame, and start not so wildly from my affair.

---

281 *recorders* musical instruments of the flute class   283 *perdy* by God
('par dieu')   289 *distempered* out of temper, vexed (twisted by Hamlet
into 'deranged')   291 *choler* anger (twisted by Hamlet into 'biliousness')
296 *frame* logical order

Hamlet. I am tame, sir; pronounce.

Guildenstern. The queen, your mother, in most great affliction of spirit hath sent me to you.

300 *Hamlet.* You are welcome.

Guildenstern. Nay, good my lord, this courtesy is not of the
right breed. If it shall please you to make me a wholesome
answer, I will do your mother's commandment. If not,
your pardon and my return shall be the end of my
305 business.

Hamlet. Sir, I cannot.

Rosencrantz. What, my lord?

Hamlet. Make you a wholesome answer; my wit's diseased.
But, sir, such answer as I can make, you shall command,
310 or rather, as you say, my mother. Therefore no more, but
to the matter. My mother, you say —

Rosencrantz. Then thus she says: your behavior hath struck
her into amazement and admiration.

Hamlet. O wonderful son, that can so stonish a mother! But
315 is there no sequel at the heels of this mother's admiration?
Impart.

Rosencrantz. She desires to speak with you in her closet ere
you go to bed.

Hamlet. We shall obey, were she ten times our mother.
320 Have you any further trade with us?

Rosencrantz. My lord, you once did love me.

Hamlet. And do still, by these pickers and stealers.

Rosencrantz. Good my lord, what is your cause of distemper? You do surely bar the door upon your own
325 liberty, if you deny your griefs to your friend.

Hamlet. Sir, I lack advancement.

313 *admiration* wonder   317 *closet* private room   322 *pickers and stealers*
i.e. hands

106

Rosencrantz. How can that be, when you have the voice of
the king himself for your succession in Denmark?

Hamlet. Ay, sir, but 'while the grass grows' — the proverb is
something musty.   330

Enter the Player with recorders.

O, the recorders. Let me see one. To withdraw with you —
why do you go about to recover the wind of me, as if you
would drive me into a toil?

Guildenstern. O my lord, if my duty be too bold, my love is
too unmannerly.   335

Hamlet. I do not well understand that. Will you play upon
this pipe?

Guildenstern. My lord, I cannot.

Hamlet. I pray you.

Guildenstern. Believe me, I cannot.   340

Hamlet. I do beseech you.

Guildenstern. I know no touch of it, my lord.

Hamlet. It is as easy as lying. Govern these ventages with
your fingers and thumb, give it breath with your mouth,
and it will discourse most eloquent music. Look you,   345
these are the stops.

Guildenstern. But these cannot I command to any utt'rance
of harmony. I have not the skill.

Hamlet. Why, look you now, how unworthy a thing you
make of me! You would play upon me, you would seem   350
to know my stops, you would pluck out the heart of my
mystery, you would sound me from my lowest note to

329 *while the grass grows* (a proverb, ending: 'the horse starves') 331 *recorders* (see III, ii, 281) *withdraw* step aside 332 *recover the wind* come up
to windward like a hunter 333 *toil* snare 334–35 *is too unmannerly*
leads me beyond the restraint of good manners 343 *ventages* holes, vents

the top of my compass; and there is much music, excellent
voice, in this little organ, yet cannot you make it speak.
355 'Sblood, do you think I am easier to be played on than a
pipe? Call me what instrument you will, though you can
fret me, you cannot play upon me.

Enter Polonius.

God bless you, sir!
Polonius. My lord, the queen would speak with you, and
360 presently.
Hamlet. Do you see yonder cloud that's almost in shape of a
camel?
Polonius. By th' mass and 'tis, like a camel indeed.
Hamlet. Methinks it is like a weasel.
365 *Polonius.* It is backed like a weasel.
Hamlet. Or like a whale.
Polonius. Very like a whale.
Hamlet. Then I will come to my mother by and by.
[*aside*] They fool me to the top of my bent. — I will come
370 by and by.
Polonius. I will say so.   [*Exit.*]
Hamlet. 'By and by' is easily said. Leave me, friends.
                                        [*Exeunt all but Hamlet.*]
'Tis now the very witching time of night,
When churchyards yawn, and hell itself breathes out
375 Contagion to this world. Now could I drink hot blood
And do such bitter business as the day
Would quake to look on. Soft, now to my mother.
O heart, lose not thy nature; let not ever
The soul of Nero enter this firm bosom.

357 *fret* irritate (with a play on the fret-fingering of certain stringed
musical instruments) 360 *presently* at once 368 *by and by* immediately
369 *bent* (see II, ii, 30) 379 *Nero* murderer of his mother

Let me be cruel, not unnatural;   380
I will speak daggers to her, but use none.
My tongue and soul in this be hypocrites:
How in my words somever she be shent,
To give them seals never, my soul, consent!   *Exit.*

❀

Enter King, Rosencrantz, and Guildenstern.   III, iii

King. I like him not, nor stands it safe with us
  To let his madness range. Therefore prepare you.
  I your commission will forthwith dispatch,
  And he to England shall along with you.
  The terms of our estate may not endure   5
  Hazard so near's as doth hourly grow
  Out of his brows.
Guildenstern.   We will ourselves provide.
  Most holy and religious fear it is
  To keep those many many bodies safe
  That live and feed upon your majesty.   10
Rosencrantz. The single and peculiar life is bound
  With all the strength and armor of the mind
  To keep itself from noyance, but much more
  That spirit upon whose weal depends and rests
  The lives of many. The cess of majesty   15
  Dies not alone, but like a gulf doth draw
  What's near it with it; or 'tis a massy wheel
  Fixed on the summit of the highest mount,

383 *shent* reproved   384 *seals* authentications in actions   III, iii, 5 *terms*
circumstances   *estate* royal position   7 *brows* effronteries (apparently with
an implication of knitted brows)   11 *peculiar* individual   13 *noyance* harm
15 *cess* cessation, decease   16 *gulf* whirlpool

To whose huge spokes ten thousand lesser things

20 Are mortised and adjoined, which when it falls,
Each small annexment, petty consequence,
Attends the boist'rous ruin. Never alone
Did the king sigh, but with a general groan.

King. Arm you, I pray you, to this speedy voyage,

25 For we will fetters put upon this fear,
Which now goes too free-footed.

Rosencrantz.   We will haste us.

Exeunt Gentlemen

Enter Polonius.

Polonius. My lord, he's going to his mother's closet.
Behind the arras I'll convey myself
To hear the process. I'll warrant she'll tax him home.

30 And, as you said, and wisely was it said,
'Tis meet that some more audience than a mother,
Since nature makes them partial, should o'erhear
The speech, of vantage. Fare you well, my liege.
I'll call upon you ere you go to bed
And tell you what I know.

35 *King.*   Thanks, dear my lord.

Exit [Polonius].

O, my offense is rank, it smells to heaven;
It hath the primal eldest curse upon't,
A brother's murther. Pray can I not,
Though inclination be as sharp as will.

40 My stronger guilt defeats my strong intent,
And like a man to double business bound

---

22 *Attends* joins in (like a royal attendant)   24 *Arm* prepare   29 *process*
proceedings   *tax him home* thrust home in reprimanding him   33 *of vantage*
from an advantageous position   37 *primal eldest curse* that of Cain, who also
murdered a brother

I stand in pause where I shall first begin,
And both neglect. What if this cursèd hand
Were thicker than itself with brother's blood,
Is there not rain enough in the sweet heavens   45
To wash it white as snow? Whereto serves mercy
But to confront the visage of offense?
And what's in prayer but this twofold force,
To be forestallèd ere we come to fall,
Or pardoned being down? Then I'll look up.   50
My fault is past. But, O, what form of prayer
Can serve my turn? 'Forgive me my foul murther'?
That cannot be, since I am still possessed
Of those effects for which I did the murther,
My crown, mine own ambition, and my queen.   55
May one be pardoned and retain th' offense?
In the corrupted currents of this world
Offense's gilded hand may shove by justice,
And oft 'tis seen the wicked prize itself
Buys out the law. But 'tis not so above.   60
There is no shuffling; there the action lies
In his true nature, and we ourselves compelled,
Even to the teeth and forehead of our faults,
To give in evidence. What then? What rests?
Try what repentance can. What can it not?   65
Yet what can it when one cannot repent?
O wretched state! O bosom black as death!
O limèd soul, that struggling to be free
Art more engaged! Help, angels! Make assay.
Bow, stubborn knees, and, heart with strings of steel, 70

47 *offense* sin   54 *effects* things acquired   58 *gilded* gold-laden   61 *shuffling* sharp practice, double-dealing   *action* legal proceeding (in heaven's court)   63 *teeth and forehead* face-to-face recognition   68 *limèd* caught in birdlime, a gluey material spread as a bird-snare   69 *engaged* embedded   *assay* an attempt

Be soft as sinews of the new-born babe.
All may be well.   *[He kneels.]*

Enter Hamlet.

Hamlet. Now might I do it pat, now 'a is a-praying,
And now I'll do't. And so 'a goes to heaven,
75   And so am I revenged. That would be scanned.
A villain kills my father, and for that
I, his sole son, do this same villain send
To heaven.
Why, this is hire and salary, not revenge.
80   'A took my father grossly, full of bread,
With all his crimes broad blown, as flush as May;
And how his audit stands, who knows save heaven?
But in our circumstance and course of thought,
'Tis heavy with him; and am I then revenged,
85   To take him in the purging of his soul,
When he is fit and seasoned for his passage?
No.
Up, sword, and know thou a more horrid hent.
When he is drunk asleep, or in his rage,
90   Or in th' incestuous pleasure of his bed,
At game a-swearing, or about some act
That has no relish of salvation in't —
Then trip him, that his heels may kick at heaven,
And that his soul may be as damned and black
95   As hell, whereto it goes. My mother stays.
This physic but prolongs thy sickly days.   *Exit.*

73 *pat* opportunely 80 *grossly* in a state of gross unpreparedness *bread*
i.e. worldly sense gratification 81 *broad blown* fully blossomed *flush* vig-
orous 82 *audit* account 88 *more horrid hent* grasping by me on a more
horrid occasion 92 *relish* flavor

King. [rises] My words fly up, my thoughts remain below.
  Words without thoughts never to heaven go.   *Exit.*

❀

Enter [Queen] Gertrude and Polonius.   III, iv

Polonius. 'A will come straight. Look you lay home to him.
  Tell him his pranks have been too broad to bear with,
  And that your grace hath screened and stood between
  Much heat and him. I'll silence me even here.
  Pray you be round with him.   5
[*Hamlet. (within)* Mother, mother, mother!]
Queen. I'll warrant you; fear me not. Withdraw; I hear
  him coming.   [*Polonius hides behind the arras.*]

Enter Hamlet.

Hamlet. Now, mother, what's the matter?
Queen. Hamlet, thou hast thy father much offended.   10
Hamlet. Mother, you have my father much offended.
Queen. Come, come, you answer with an idle tongue.
Hamlet. Go, go, you question with a wicked tongue.
Queen. Why, how now, Hamlet?
Hamlet.   What's the matter now?
Queen. Have you forgot me?
Hamlet.   No, by the rood, not so!   15
  You are the queen, your husband's brother's wife,
  And (would it were not so) you are my mother.
Queen. Nay, then I'll set those to you that can speak.
Hamlet. Come, come, and sit you down. You shall not
    budge.

III, iv, 1 *lay* thrust 2 *broad* unrestrained 5 *round* plain-spoken 12 *idle*
foolish 15 *rood* cross

113

20   You go not till I set you up a glass
      Where you may see the inmost part of you.
      Queen. What wilt thou do? Thou wilt not murther me?
      Help, ho!
      Polonius. [behind] What, ho! help!
25 *Hamlet.* [draws] How now? a rat? Dead for a ducat, dead!
                      [*Makes a pass through the arras and kills Polonius.*]
      Polonius. [behind] O, I am slain!
      Queen.   O me, what hast thou done?
      Hamlet. Nay, I know not. Is it the king?
      Queen. O, what a rash and bloody deed is this!
      Hamlet. A bloody deed — almost as bad, good mother,
30   As kill a king, and marry with his brother.
      Queen. As kill a king?
      Hamlet.   Ay, lady, it was my word.
                         [*Lifts up the arras and sees Polonius.*]
      Thou wretched, rash, intruding fool, farewell!
      I took thee for thy better. Take thy fortune.
      Thou find'st to be too busy is some danger. —
35   Leave wringing of your hands. Peace, sit you down
      And let me wring your heart, for so I shall
      If it be made of penetrable stuff,
      If damnèd custom have not brazed it so
      That it is proof and bulwark against sense.
40 *Queen.* What have I done that thou dar'st wag thy tongue
      In noise so rude against me?
      Hamlet.   Such an act
      That blurs the grace and blush of modesty,
      Calls virtue hypocrite, takes off the rose
      From the fair forehead of an innocent love,
45   And sets a blister there, makes marriage vows

---

38 *custom* habit   *brazed* hardened like brass   39 *proof* armor   *sense* feeling
45 *blister* brand (of degradation)

As false as dicers' oaths. O, such a deed
As from the body of contraction plucks
The very soul, and sweet religion makes
A rhapsody of words! Heaven's face does glow,
And this solidity and compound mass,   50
With heated visage, as against the doom,
Is thought-sick at the act.

Queen.   Ay me, what act,
That roars so loud and thunders in the index?

Hamlet. Look here upon this picture, and on this,
The counterfeit presentment of two brothers.   55
See what a grace was seated on this brow:
Hyperion's curls, the front of Jove himself,
An eye like Mars, to threaten and command,
A station like the herald Mercury
New lighted on a heaven-kissing hill —   60
A combination and a form indeed
Where every god did seem to set his seal
To give the world assurance of a man.
This was your husband. Look you now what follows.
Here is your husband, like a mildewed ear   65
Blasting his wholesome brother. Have you eyes?
Could you on this fair mountain leave to feed,
And batten on this moor? Ha! have you eyes?
You cannot call it love, for at your age
The heyday in the blood is tame, it's humble,   70
And waits upon the judgment, and what judgment

47 *contraction* the marriage contract   48 *religion* i.e. sacred marriage vows
50 *compound mass* the earth as compounded of the four elements   51 *against*
in expectation of   *doom* Day of Judgment   53 *index* table of contents preceding the body of a book   55 *counterfeit presentment* portrayed representation   57 *Hyperion* the sun god   *front* forehead   59 *station* attitude in
standing   68 *batten* feed greedily   70 *heyday* excitement of passion
71 *waits upon* yields to

Would step from this to this? Sense sure you have,
Else could you not have motion, but sure that sense
Is apoplexed, for madness would not err,
75   Nor sense to ecstasy was ne'er so thralled
But it reserved some quantity of choice
To serve in such a difference. What devil was't
That thus hath cozened you at hoodman-blind?
Eyes without feeling, feeling without sight,
80   Ears without hands or eyes, smelling sans all,
Or but a sickly part of one true sense
Could not so mope.
O shame, where is thy blush? Rebellious hell,
If thou canst mutine in a matron's bones,
85   To flaming youth let virtue be as wax
And melt in her own fire. Proclaim no shame
When the compulsive ardor gives the charge,
Since frost itself as actively doth burn,
And reason panders will.

Queen.   O Hamlet, speak no more.
90   Thou turn'st mine eyes into my very soul,
And there I see such black and grainèd spots
As will not leave their tinct.

Hamlet.   Nay, but to live
In the rank sweat of an enseamèd bed,
Stewed in corruption, honeying and making love
Over the nasty sty —

95 *Queen.*   O, speak to me no more.
These words like daggers enter in mine ears.
No more, sweet Hamlet.

72 *Sense* feeling 73 *motion* desire, impulse 74 *apoplexed* paralyzed 75 *ecstasy* madness 78 *cozened* cheated *hoodman-blind* blindman's buff 80 *sans* without 82 *mope* be stupid 84 *mutine* mutiny 87 *compulsive* compelling *gives the charge* delivers the attack 89 *panders will* acts as procurer for desire 91 *grainèd* dyed in grain 92 *tinct* color 93 *enseamèd* grease-laden

Hamlet.   A murtherer and a villain,
   A slave that is not twentieth part the tithe
   Of your precedent lord, a vice of kings,
   A cutpurse of the empire and the rule,   100
   That from a shelf the precious diadem stole
   And put it in his pocket —
Queen.   No more.

          Enter [the] Ghost [in his nightgown].

Hamlet. A king of shreds and patches —
   Save me and hover o'er me with your wings,
   You heavenly guards! What would your gracious figure? 105
Queen. Alas, he's mad.
Hamlet. Do you not come your tardy son to chide,
   That, lapsed in time and passion, lets go by
   Th' important acting of your dread command?
   O, say!   110
Ghost. Do not forget. This visitation
   Is but to whet thy almost blunted purpose.
   But look, amazement on thy mother sits.
   O, step between her and her fighting soul!
   Conceit in weakest bodies strongest works.   115
   Speak to her, Hamlet.
Hamlet.   How is it with you, lady?
Queen. Alas, how is't with you,
   That you do bend your eye on vacancy,
   And with th' incorporal air do hold discourse?
   Forth at your eyes your spirits wildly peep,   120

---

98 *tithe* tenth part 99 *vice* clownish rogue (like the Vice of the morality
plays) 100 *cutpurse* skulking thief 102 s.d. *nightgown* dressing gown
108 *lapsed . . . passion* having let the moment slip and passion cool 115 *Conceit* imagination 119 *incorporal* bodiless

And as the sleeping soldiers in th' alarm
Your bedded hairs like life in excrements
Start up and stand an end. O gentle son,
Upon the heat and flame of thy distemper

125   Sprinkle cool patience. Whereon do you look?
Hamlet. On him, on him! Look you, how pale he glares!
His form and cause conjoined, preaching to stones,
Would make them capable. — Do not look upon
   me,
Lest with this piteous action you convert

130   My stern effects. Then what I have to do
Will want true color — tears perchance for blood.
Queen. To whom do you speak this?
Hamlet.   Do you see nothing there?
Queen. Nothing at all; yet all that is I see.
Hamlet. Nor did you nothing hear?
Queen.   No, nothing but ourselves.

135   *Hamlet.* Why, look you there! Look how it steals away!
My father, in his habit as he lived!
Look where he goes even now out at the portal!

                                        Exit Ghost.

Queen. This is the very coinage of your brain.
This bodiless creation ecstasy
Is very cunning in.

140   *Hamlet.*   Ecstasy?
My pulse as yours doth temperately keep time
And makes as healthful music. It is not madness
That I have uttered. Bring me to the test,
And I the matter will reword, which madness

145   Would gambol from. Mother, for love of grace,

122 *excrements* outgrowths   123 *an* on   124 *distemper* mental disorder
128 *capable* susceptible   130 *effects* manifestations of emotion and purpose
139 *ecstasy* madness   145 *gambol* shy (like a startled horse)

Lay not that flattering unction to your soul,
That not your trespass but my madness speaks.
It will but skin and film the ulcerous place
Whiles rank corruption, mining all within,
Infects unseen. Confess yourself to heaven,   150
Repent what's past, avoid what is to come,
And do not spread the compost on the weeds
To make them ranker. Forgive me this my virtue.
For in the fatness of these pursy times
Virtue itself of vice must pardon beg,   155
Yea, curb and woo for leave to do him good.
Queen. O Hamlet, thou hast cleft my heart in twain.
Hamlet. O, throw away the worser part of it,
And live the purer with the other half.
Good night — but go not to my uncle's bed.   160
Assume a virtue, if you have it not.
That monster custom, who all sense doth eat,
Of habits devil, is angel yet in this,
That to the use of actions fair and good
He likewise gives a frock or livery   165
That aptly is put on. Refrain to-night,
And that shall lend a kind of easiness
To the next abstinence; the next more easy;
For use almost can change the stamp of nature,
And either . . . the devil, or throw him out   170
With wondrous potency. Once more, good night,
And when you are desirous to be blest,
I'll blessing beg of you. — For this same lord,

146 *unction* ointment   149 *mining* undermining   152 *compost* fertilizing
mixture   154 *fatness* gross slackness   *pursy* corpulent   156 *curb* bow to
162–63 *all sense . . . devil* (see Supplementary Notes, pp. 175–76)   165 *livery* characteristic dress (accompanying the suggestion of 'garb' in *habits*)
169 *use* habit   *stamp* impression, form   170 *And . . . out* (see Supplementary Notes, p. 176)

I do repent; but heaven hath pleased it so,
175 To punish me with this, and this with me,
That I must be their scourge and minister.
I will bestow him and will answer well
The death I gave him. So again, good night.
I must be cruel only to be kind.
180 Thus bad begins, and worse remains behind.
One word more, good lady.

Queen.   What shall I do?

Hamlet. Not this, by no means, that I bid you do:
Let the bloat king tempt you again to bed,
Pinch wanton on your cheek, call you his mouse,
185 And let him, for a pair of reechy kisses,
Or paddling in your neck with his damned fingers,
Make you to ravel all this matter out,
That I essentially am not in madness,
But mad in craft. 'Twere good you let him know,
190 For who that's but a queen, fair, sober, wise,
Would from a paddock, from a bat, a gib,
Such dear concernings hide? Who would do so?
No, in despite of sense and secrecy,
Unpeg the basket on the house's top,
195 Let the birds fly, and like the famous ape,
To try conclusions, in the basket creep
And break your own neck down.

Queen. Be thou assured, if words be made of breath,
And breath of life, I have no life to breathe
200 What thou hast said to me.

---

177 *bestow* stow, hide   180 *behind* to come   183 *bloat* bloated with sense
gratification   185 *reechy* filthy   187 *ravel . . . out* disentangle   191 *paddock*
toad   *gib* tomcat   192 *dear concernings* matters of great personal significance
195 *famous ape* (one in a story now unknown)   196 *conclusions* experiments

Hamlet. I must to England; you know that?
Queen.   Alack,
    I had forgot. 'Tis so concluded on.
Hamlet. There's letters sealed, and my two schoolfellows,
    Whom I will trust as I will adders fanged,
    They bear the mandate; they must sweep my way   205
    And marshal me to knavery. Let it work.
    For 'tis the sport to have the enginer
    Hoist with his own petar, and 't shall go hard
    But I will delve one yard below their mines
    And blow them at the moon. O, 'tis most sweet   210
    When in one line two crafts directly meet.
    This man shall set me packing.
    I'll lug the guts into the neighbor room.
    Mother, good night. Indeed, this counsellor
    Is now most still, most secret, and most grave,   215
    Who was in life a foolish prating knave.
    Come, sir, to draw toward an end with you.
    Good night, mother.
                    [*Exit the Queen. Then*] *exit* [*Hamlet, tugging in
                                                    Polonius*].

❦

205 *mandate* order 207 *enginer* engineer, constructor of military engines
or works 208 *Hoist* blown up *petar* petard, bomb or mine 212 *packing*
travelling in a hurry (with a play upon his 'packing' or shouldering of
Polonius' body and also upon his 'packing' in the sense of 'plotting' or
'contriving')

IV, i   *Enter King and Queen, with Rosencrantz and Guildenstern.*

King. There's matter in these sighs. These profound heaves
     You must translate; 'tis fit we understand them.
     Where is your son?
Queen. Bestow this place on us a little while.
                       [Exeunt Rosencrantz and Guildenstern.]
5   Ah, mine own lord, what have I seen to-night!
King. What, Gertrude? How does Hamlet?
Queen. Mad as the sea and wind when both contend
     Which is the mightier. In his lawless fit,
     Behind the arras hearing something stir,
10   Whips out his rapier, cries, 'A rat, a rat!'
     And in this brainish apprehension kills
     The unseen good old man.
King.   O heavy deed!
     It had been so with us, had we been there.
     His liberty is full of threats to all,
15   To you yourself, to us, to every one.
     Alas, how shall this bloody deed be answered?
     It will be laid to us, whose providence
     Should have kept short, restrained, and out of haunt
     This mad young man. But so much was our love
20   We would not understand what was most fit,
     But, like the owner of a foul disease,
     To keep it from divulging, let it feed
     Even on the pith of life. Where is he gone?
Queen. To draw apart the body he hath killed;
25   O'er whom his very madness, like some ore
     Among a mineral of metals base,
     Shows itself pure. 'A weeps for what is done.

IV, i, 11 *brainish apprehension* headstrong conception   17 *providence* fore-sight   18 *haunt* association with others   22 *divulging* becoming known
25 *ore* vein of gold   26 *mineral* mine

King. O Gertrude, come away!
  The sun no sooner shall the mountains touch
  But we will ship him hence, and this vile deed   30
  We must with all our majesty and skill
  Both countenance and excuse. Ho, Guildenstern!

Enter Rosencrantz and Guildenstern.

  Friends both, go join you with some further aid.
  Hamlet in madness hath Polonius slain,
  And from his mother's closet hath he dragged him.   35
  Go seek him out; speak fair, and bring the body
  Into the chapel. I pray you haste in this.
              [Exeunt Rosencrantz and Guildenstern.]
  Come, Gertrude, we'll call up our wisest friends
  And let them know both what we mean to do
  And what's untimely done . . .   '40
  Whose whisper o'er the world's diameter,
  As level as the cannon to his blank
  Transports his poisoned shot, may miss our name
  And hit the woundless air. O, come away!
  My soul is full of discord and dismay.   *Exeunt.* 45

Enter Hamlet.   IV, ii

Hamlet. Safely stowed.
Gentlemen. (*within*) Hamlet! Lord Hamlet!
Hamlet. But soft, what noise? Who calls on Hamlet? O,
  here they come.

40 *And . . . done* (see Supplementary Notes, p. 176) 42 *As level* with as
direct aim *blank* mark, central white spot on a target

[Enter] Rosencrantz, [Guildenstern,] and others.

Rosencrantz. What have you done, my lord, with the dead
5   body?

Hamlet. Compounded it with dust, whereto 'tis kin.

Rosencrantz. Tell us where 'tis, that we may take it thence
    And bear it to the chapel.

Hamlet. Do not believe it.

10 *Rosencrantz.* Believe what?

Hamlet. That I can keep your counsel and not mine own.
    Besides, to be demanded of a sponge, what replication
    should be made by the son of a king?

Rosencrantz. Take you me for a sponge, my lord?

15 *Hamlet.* Ay, sir, that soaks up the king's countenance, his
    rewards, his authorities. But such officers do the king best
    service in the end. He keeps them, like an ape, in the
    corner of his jaw, first mouthed, to be last swallowed.
    When he needs what you have gleaned, it is but squeezing
20   you and, sponge, you shall be dry again.

Rosencrantz. I understand you not, my lord.

Hamlet. I am glad of it. A knavish speech sleeps in a foolish
    ear.

Rosencrantz. My lord, you must tell us where the body is
25   and go with us to the king.

Hamlet. The body is with the king, but the king is not with
    the body. The king is a thing —

Guildenstern. A thing, my lord?

Hamlet. Of nothing. Bring me to him. Hide fox, and all
30   after.   *Exeunt.*

❁

IV, ii, 12 *replication* reply 15 *countenance* favor 22 *sleeps in* means
nothing to 29 *Of nothing* (cf. Prayer Book, Psalm 144: 4, 'Man is like a
thing of naught: his time passeth away like a shadow') 29–30 *Hide ...
after* (apparently well-known words from some game of hide-and-seek)

Enter King, and two or three.   IV, iii

King. I have sent to seek him and to find the body.
How dangerous is it that this man goes loose!
Yet must not we put the strong law on him;
He's loved of the distracted multitude,
Who like not in their judgment, but their eyes,   5
And where 'tis so, th' offender's scourge is weighed,
But never the offense. To bear all smooth and even,
This sudden sending him away must seem
Deliberate pause. Diseases desperate grown
By desperate appliance are relieved,   10
Or not at all.

Enter Rosencrantz, [Guildenstern,] and all the rest.

How now? What hath befallen?
Rosencrantz. Where the dead body is bestowed, my lord,
We cannot get from him.
King.   But where is he?
Rosencrantz. Without, my lord; guarded, to know your
    pleasure.
King. Bring him before us.
Rosencrantz.   Ho! Bring in the lord.   15

They enter [with Hamlet].

King. Now, Hamlet, where's Polonius?
Hamlet. At supper.
King. At supper? Where?
Hamlet. Not where he eats, but where 'a is eaten. A
    certain convocation of politic worms are e'en at him. 20

IV, iii, 4 *distracted* confused   6 *scourge* punishment   9 *Deliberate pause*
something done with much deliberation   20 *politic worms* political and
craftily scheming worms (such as Polonius might well attract)

Your worm is your only emperor for diet. We fat
all creatures else to fat us, and we fat ourselves for
maggots. Your fat king and your lean beggar is but
variable service — two dishes, but to one table. That's
25 the end.

King. Alas, alas!

Hamlet. A man may fish with the worm that hath eat of a
king, and eat of the fish that hath fed of that worm.

King. What dost thou mean by this?

30 *Hamlet.* Nothing but to show you how a king may go a
progress through the guts of a beggar.

King. Where is Polonius?

Hamlet. In heaven. Send thither to see. If your messenger
find him not there, seek him i' th' other place yourself.
35 But if indeed you find him not within this month, you
shall nose him as you go up the stairs into the lobby.

King. *[to Attendants]* Go seek him there.

Hamlet. 'A will stay till you come.   *[Exeunt Attendants.]*

King. Hamlet, this deed, for thine especial safety,
40 Which we do tender as we dearly grieve
For that which thou hast done, must send thee hence
With fiery quickness. Therefore prepare thyself.
The bark is ready and the wind at help,
Th' associates tend, and everything is bent
For England.

Hamlet.   For England?

King.   Ay, Hamlet.

---

21 *diet* food and drink (perhaps with a play upon a famous 'convocation,'
the Diet of Worms opened by the Emperor Charles V on January 28, 1521,
before which Luther appeared) 24 *variable service* different servings of one
food 31 *progress* royal journey of state 40 *tender* hold dear *dearly* intense-
ly 44 *tend* wait *bent* set in readiness (like a bent bow)

Hamlet.   Good.   45
King. So is it, if thou knew'st our purposes.
Hamlet. I see a cherub that sees them. But come, for Eng-
  land! Farewell, dear mother.
King. Thy loving father, Hamlet.
Hamlet. My mother — father and mother is man and wife, 50
  man and wife is one flesh, and so, my mother. Come, for
  England!   *Exit.*
King. Follow him at foot; tempt him with speed aboard.
  Delay it not; I'll have him hence to-night.
  Away! for everything is sealed and done   55
  That else leans on th' affair. Pray you make haste.
                          [Exeunt all but the King.]
  And, England, if my love thou hold'st at aught —
  As my great power thereof may give thee sense,
  Since yet thy cicatrice looks raw and red
  After the Danish sword, and thy free awe   60
  Pays homage to us — thou mayst not coldly set
  Our sovereign process, which imports at full
  By letters congruing to that effect
  The present death of Hamlet. Do it, England,
  For like the hectic in my blood he rages,   65
  And thou must cure me. Till I know 'tis done,
  Howe'er my haps, my joys were ne'er begun.   *Exit.*

❀

47 *cherub* one of the cherubim (angels with a distinctive quality of knowledge) 53 *at foot* at heel, close 56 *leans on* is connected with 57 *England*
King of England 60 *free awe* voluntary show of respect 61 *set* esteem
62 *process* formal command 63 *congruing* agreeing 64 *present* instant
65 *hectic* a continuous fever 67 *haps* fortunes

Enter Fortinbras with his Army over the stage.

Fortinbras. Go, captain, from me greet the Danish king.
　　Tell him that by his license Fortinbras
　　Craves the conveyance of a promised march
　　Over his kingdom. You know the rendezvous.
5　　If that his majesty would aught with us,
　　We shall express our duty in his eye;
　　And let him know so.
Captain.　　　　　　　I will do't, my lord.
Fortinbras. Go softly on.　　　*[Exeunt all but the Captain.]*

　　Enter Hamlet, Rosencrantz, [Guildenstern,] and others.

Hamlet. Good sir, whose powers are these?
10 *Captain.* They are of Norway, sir.
Hamlet. How purposed, sir, I pray you?
Captain. Against some part of Poland.
Hamlet. Who commands them, sir?
Captain. The nephew to old Norway, Fortinbras.
15 *Hamlet.* Goes it against the main of Poland, sir,
　　Or for some frontier?
Captain. Truly to speak, and with no addition,
　　We go to gain a little patch of ground
　　That hath in it no profit but the name.
20　　To pay five ducats, five, I would not farm it,
　　Nor will it yield to Norway or the Pole
　　A ranker rate, should it be sold in fee.
Hamlet. Why, then the Polack never will defend it.
Captain. Yes, it is already garrisoned.
25 *Hamlet.* Two thousand souls and twenty thousand ducats

IV, iv, 3 *conveyance* escort   6 *eye* presence   8 *softly* slowly   9 *powers*
forces   15 *main* main body   17 *addition* exaggeration   20 *To pay* i.e. for a
yearly rental of   22 *ranker* more abundant   *in fee* outright

Will not debate the question of this straw.
This is th' imposthume of much wealth and peace,
That inward breaks, and shows no cause without
Why the man dies. I humbly thank you, sir.
Captain. God bye you, sir.   *[Exit.]*
Rosencrantz.   Will't please you go, my lord? 30
Hamlet. I'll be with you straight. Go a little before.
                                   [Exeunt all but Hamlet.]
How all occasions do inform against me
And spur my dull revenge! What is a man,
If his chief good and market of his time
Be but to sleep and feed? A beast, no more.   35
Sure he that made us with such large discourse,
Looking before and after, gave us not
That capability and godlike reason
To fust in us unused. Now, whether it be
Bestial oblivion, or some craven scruple   40
Of thinking too precisely on th' event —
A thought which, quartered, hath but one part wisdom
And ever three parts coward — I do not know
Why yet I live to say, 'This thing's to do,'
Sith I have cause, and will, and strength, and means   45
To do't. Examples gross as earth exhort me.
Witness this army of such mass and charge,
Led by a delicate and tender prince,
Whose spirit, with divine ambition puffed,
Makes mouths at the invisible event,   50
Exposing what is mortal and unsure
To all that fortune, death, and danger dare,

27 *imposthume* abscess   32 *inform* take shape   34 *market of* compensation
for   36 *discourse* power of thought   39 *fust* grow mouldy   40 *oblivion*
forgetfulness   41 *event* outcome (as also in line 50)   46 *gross* large and
evident   47 *charge* expense   50 *Makes mouths* makes faces scornfully

Even for an eggshell. Rightly to be great
Is not to stir without great argument,
55   But greatly to find quarrel in a straw
When honor's at the stake. How stand I then,
That have a father killed, a mother stained,
Excitements of my reason and my blood,
And let all sleep, while to my shame I see
60   The imminent death of twenty thousand men
That for a fantasy and trick of fame
Go to their graves like beds, fight for a plot
Whereon the numbers cannot try the cause,
Which is not tomb enough and continent
65   To hide the slain? O, from this time forth,
My thoughts be bloody, or be nothing worth!   *Exit.*

❈

IV, v   *Enter Horatio, [Queen] Gertrude, and a Gentleman.*

Queen. I will not speak with her.
Gentleman. She is importunate, indeed distract.
Her mood will needs be pitied.
Queen.   What would she have?
Gentleman. She speaks much of her father, says she hears
5   There's tricks i' th' world, and hems, and beats her heart,
Spurns enviously at straws, speaks things in doubt
That carry but half sense. Her speech is nothing,
Yet the unshapèd use of it doth move
The hearers to collection; they aim at it,

55 *greatly . . . straw* to recognize the great argument even in some small
matter   61 *fantasy* fanciful image   *trick* toy   63 *try the cause* find space in
which to settle the issue by battle   64 *continent* receptacle   IV, v, 2 *distract*
insane   5 *tricks* deceits   6 *Spurns enviously* kicks spitefully, takes offense
straws trifles   8 *unshapèd use* disordered manner   9 *collection* attempts at
shaping meaning   *aim* guess

And botch the words up fit to their own thoughts,   10
Which, as her winks and nods and gestures yield them,
Indeed would make one think there might be thought,
Though nothing sure, yet much unhappily.
Horatio. 'Twere good she were spoken with, for she may strew
Dangerous conjectures in ill-breeding minds.   15
Queen. Let her come in.   [*Exit Gentleman.*]
[*Aside*] To my sick soul (as sin's true nature is)
Each toy seems prologue to some great amiss.
So full of artless jealousy is guilt
It spills itself in fearing to be spilt.   20

Enter Ophelia [distracted].

Ophelia. Where is the beauteous majesty of Denmark?
Queen. How now, Ophelia?
Ophelia. How should I your true-love know   *She sings.*
          From another one?
          By his cockle hat and staff   25
          And his sandal shoon.
Queen. Alas, sweet lady, what imports this song?
Ophelia. Say you? Nay, pray you mark.
          He is dead and gone, lady,   (*Song.*)
          He is dead and gone;   30
          At his head a grass-green turf,
          At his heels a stone.
    O, ho!
Queen. Nay, but Ophelia —

10 *botch* patch 18 *toy* trifle *amiss* calamity 19 *artless* unskillfully managed *jealousy* suspicion 20 *spills* destroys 25 *cockle hat* hat bearing a cockle shell, worn by a pilgrim who had been to the shrine of St. James of Compostela 26 *shoon* shoes

35 *Ophelia.* Pray you mark.
  [Sings] White his shroud as the mountain snow —

                    Enter King.

Queen. Alas, look here, my lord.
Ophelia.   Larded all with sweet flowers;   (Song.)
              Which bewept to the grave did not go
40   With true-love showers.
King. How do you, pretty lady?
Ophelia. Well, God dild you! They say the owl was a
   baker's daughter. Lord, we know what we are, but know
   not what we may be. God be at your table!
45 *King.* Conceit upon her father.
Ophelia. Pray let's have no words of this, but when they
   ask you what it means, say you this:
              To-morrow is Saint Valentine's day.   (Song.)
              All in the morning betime,
50   And I a maid at your window,
              To be your Valentine.

              Then up he rose and donned his clo'es
              And dupped the chamber door,
              Let in the maid, that out a maid
55   Never departed more.
King. Pretty Ophelia!
Ophelia. Indeed, la, without an oath, I'll make an end on't:
   [Sings] By Gis and by Saint Charity,
              Alack, and fie for shame!
60   Young men will do't if they come to't.
              By Cock, they are to blame.

38 *Larded* garnished 42 *dild* yield, repay *the owl* an owl into which, according to a folktale, a baker's daughter was transformed because of her
failure to show wholehearted generosity when Christ asked for bread in the
baker's shop 45 *Conceit* thought 49 *betime* early 53 *dupped* opened 58 *Gis*
Jesus 61 *Cock* God

>   Quoth she, 'Before you tumbled me,
>   You promised me to wed.'
> He answers:
>   'So would I 'a' done, by yonder sun,   65
>   An thou hadst not come to my bed.'

King. How long hath she been thus?

Ophelia. I hope all will be well. We must be patient, but I
cannot choose but weep to think they would lay him i' th'
cold ground. My brother shall know of it; and so I   70
thank you for your good counsel. Come, my coach!
Good night, ladies, good night. Sweet ladies, good
night, good night.   *[Exit.]*

King. Follow her close; give her good watch, I pray you.
                                          [Exit Horatio.]

O, this is the poison of deep grief; it springs   75
All from her father's death — and now behold!
O Gertrude, Gertrude,
When sorrows come, they come not single spies,
But in battalions: first, her father slain;
Next, your son gone, and he most violent author   80
Of his own just remove; the people muddied,
Thick and unwholesome in their thoughts and whispers
For good Polonius' death, and we have done but greenly
In hugger-mugger to inter him; poor Ophelia
Divided from herself and her fair judgment,   85
Without the which we are pictures or mere beasts;
Last, and as much containing as all these,
Her brother is in secret come from France,
Feeds on his wonder, keeps himself in clouds,
And wants not buzzers to infect his ear   90
With pestilent speeches of his father's death,

---

81 *muddied* stirred up and confused 83 *greenly* foolishly 84 *hugger-mugger*
secrecy and disorder 89 *clouds* obscurity 90 *wants* lacks *buzzers* whis-
pering talebearers

Wherein necessity, of matter beggared,
Will nothing stick our person to arraign
In ear and ear. O my dear Gertrude, this,
95   ·Like to a murd'ring piece, in many places
Gives me superfluous death.   *A noise within.*

Enter a Messenger.

Queen.   Alack, what noise is this?
King. Attend, where are my Switzers? Let them guard the
        door.
What is the matter?
Messenger.   Save yourself, my lord.
The ocean, overpeering of his list,
100   Eats not the flats with more impiteous haste
Than young Laertes, in a riotous head,
O'erbears your officers. The rabble call him lord,
And, as the world were now but to begin,
Antiquity forgot, custom not known,
105   The ratifiers and props of every word,
They cry, 'Choose we! Laertes shall be king!'
Caps, hands, and tongues applaud it to the clouds,
'Laertes shall be king! Laertes king!'   *A noise within.*
Queen. How cheerfully on the false trail they cry!
110   O, this is counter, you false Danish dogs!
King. The doors are broke.

Enter Laertes with others.

Laertes. Where is this king? — Sirs, stand you all without.
All. No, let's come in.

92 *of matter beggared* unprovided with facts   93 *nothing stick* in no way
hesitate *arraign* accuse 95 *murd'ring piece* cannon loaded with shot meant
to scatter 97 *Switzers* hired Swiss guards 99 *overpeering of* rising to look
over and pass beyond *list* boundary 100 *impiteous* pitiless 101 *head*
armed force 105 *word* promise 110 *counter* hunting backward on the trail

Laertes.   I pray you give me leave.
All. We will, we will.
Laertes. I thank you. Keep the door. *[Exeunt his Followers.]*
    O thou vile king,   115
    Give me my father.
Queen.   Calmly, good Laertes.
Laertes. That drop of blood that's calm proclaims me
    bastard,
    Cries cuckold to my father, brands the harlot
    Even here between the chaste unsmirchèd brows
    Of my true mother.
King.   What is the cause, Laertes,   120
    That thy rebellion looks so giant-like?
    Let him go, Gertrude. Do not fear our person.
    There's such divinity doth hedge a king
    That treason can but peep to what it would,
    Acts little of his will. Tell me, Laertes,   125
    Why thou art thus incensed. Let him go, Gertrude.
    Speak, man.
Laertes. Where is my father?
King.   Dead.
Queen.   But not by him.
King. Let him demand his fill.
Laertes. How came he dead? I'll not be juggled with.   130
    To hell allegiance, vows to the blackest devil,
    Conscience and grace to the profoundest pit!
    I dare damnation. To this point I stand,
    That both the worlds I give to negligence,
    Let come what comes, only I'll be revenged   135
    Most throughly for my father.

---

122 *fear* fear for   **124** *peep to* i.e. through the barrier   **134** *both the worlds* whatever may result in this world or the next   *give to negligence* disregard   **136** *throughly* thoroughly

King.   Who shall stay you?

Laertes. My will, not all the world's.
   And for my means, I'll husband them so well
   They shall go far with little.

King.   Good Laertes,
140 If you desire to know the certainty
   Of your dear father, is't writ in your revenge
   That swoopstake you will draw both friend and foe,
   Winner and loser?

Laertes. None but his enemies.

King.   Will you know them then?
145 *Laertes.* To his good friends thus wide I'll ope my arms
   And like the kind life-rend'ring pelican
   Repast them with my blood.

King.   Why, now you speak
   Like a good child and a true gentleman.
   That I am guiltless of your father's death,
150 And am most sensibly in grief for it,
   It shall as level to your judgment 'pear
   As day does to your eye.

                 A noise within: 'Let her come in.'

Laertes. How now? What noise is that?

Enter Ophelia.

   O heat, dry up my brains; tears seven times salt
155 Burn out the sense and virtue of mine eye!
   By heaven, thy madness shall be paid by weight
   Till our scale turn the beam. O rose of May,
   Dear maid, kind sister, sweet Ophelia!

---

142 *swoopstake* sweepstake, taking all stakes on the gambling table 146 *life-rend'ring* life-yielding (because the mother pelican supposedly took blood from her breast with her bill to feed her young) 150 *sensibly* feelingly 151 *level* plain 157 *beam* bar of a balance

O heavens, is't possible a young maid's wits
Should be as mortal as an old man's life?   160
[Nature is fine in love, and where 'tis fine,
It sends some precious instance of itself
After the thing it loves.]
Ophelia. They bore him barefaced on the bier   (*Song.*)
      [Hey non nony, nony, hey nony]   165
      And in his grave rained many a tear —
Fare you well, my dove!
Laertes. Hadst thou thy wits, and didst persuade revenge,
It could not move thus.
Ophelia. You must sing 'A-down a-down, and you call him   170
a-down-a.' O, how the wheel becomes it! It is the false
steward, that stole his master's daughter.
Laertes. This nothing's more than matter.
Ophelia. There's rosemary, that's for remembrance. Pray
you, love, remember. And there is pansies, that's for   175
thoughts.
Laertes. A document in madness, thoughts and remembrance
fitted.
Ophelia. There's fennel for you, and columbines. There's
rue for you, and here's some for me. We may call it herb   180
of grace o' Sundays. O, you must wear your rue with a
difference. There's a daisy. I would give you some violets,
but they withered all when my father died. They say 'a
made a good end.
  [*Sings*] For bonny sweet Robin is all my joy.   185
Laertes. Thought and affliction, passion, hell itself,
She turns to favor and to prettiness.

161 *fine* refined to purity 162 *instance* token 171 *wheel* burden, refrain
173 *more than matter* more meaningful than sane speech 177 *document* lesson 179 *fennel* symbol of flattery *columbines* symbol of thanklessness (?)
180 *rue* symbol of repentance 182 *daisy* symbol of dissembling *violets*
symbol of faithfulness 187 *favor* charm

Ophelia. And will 'a not come again?   *(Song.)*
         And will 'a not come again?
190   No, no, he is dead;
            Go to thy deathbed;
        He never will come again.

        His beard was as white as snow,
        All flaxen was his poll.
195   He is gone, he is gone,
           And we cast away moan.
          God 'a' mercy on his soul!
        And of all Christian souls, I pray God. God bye you.
                                    [Exit.]

Laertes. Do you see this, O God?
200 *King.* Laertes, I must commune with your grief,
        Or you deny me right. Go but apart,
        Make choice of whom your wisest friends you will,
        And they shall hear and judge 'twixt you and me.
        If by direct or by collateral hand
205   They find us touched, we will our kingdom give,
        Our crown, our life, and all that we call ours,
        To you in satisfaction; but if not,
        Be you content to lend your patience to us,
        And we shall jointly labor with your soul
        To give it due content.
210 *Laertes.*   Let this be so.
        His means of death, his obscure funeral —
        No trophy, sword, nor hatchment o'er his bones,
        No noble rite nor formal ostentation —
        Cry to be heard, as 'twere from heaven to earth,
        That I must call't in question.

194 *poll* head 198 *of* on 204 *collateral* indirect 205 *touched* i.e. with
the crime 212 *trophy* memorial *hatchment* coat of arms 213 *ostentation*
ceremony 215 *That* so that

King.   So you shall;   215
  And where th' offense is, let the great axe fall.
  I pray you go with me.   *Exeunt.*

❀

Enter Horatio and others.   IV, vi

Horatio. What are they that would speak with me?
Gentleman. Seafaring men, sir. They say they have letters for
  you.
Horatio. Let them come in.   *[Exit Attendant.]*
  I do not know from what part of the world   5
  I should be greeted, if not from Lord Hamlet.

Enter Sailors.

Sailor. God bless you, sir.
Horatio. Let him bless thee too.
Sailor. 'A shall, sir, an't please him. There's a letter for you,
  sir — it came from th' ambassador that was bound for   10
  England — if your name be Horatio, as I am let to know
  it is.
Horatio. *[reads the letter]* 'Horatio, when thou shalt have
  overlooked this, give these fellows some means to the
  king. They have letters for him. Ere we were two days   15
  old at sea, a pirate of very warlike appointment gave us
  chase. Finding ourselves too slow of sail, we put on a
  compelled valor, and in the grapple I boarded them. On
  the instant they got clear of our ship; so I alone became
  their prisoner. They have dealt with me like thieves of   20
  mercy, but they knew what they did: I am to do a good

IV, vi, 14 *overlooked* surveyed, scanned   *means* i.e. of access   16 *appoint-*
ment equipment   20–21 *thieves of mercy* merciful thieves

turn for them. Let the king have the letters I have sent,
and repair thou to me with as much speed as thou
wouldest fly death. I have words to speak in thine ear will
25 make thee dumb; yet are they much too light for the bore
of the matter. These good fellows will bring thee where I
am. Rosencrantz and Guildenstern hold their course for
England. Of them I have much to tell thee. Farewell.

        'He that thou knowest thine, HAMLET.'

30 Come, I will give you way for these your letters,
And do't the speedier that you may direct me
To him from whom you brought them.   *Exeunt.*

      ❀

Enter King and Laertes.

King. Now must your conscience my acquittance seal,
   And you must put me in your heart for friend,
   Sith you have heard, and with a knowing ear,
   That he which hath your noble father slain
   Pursued my life.
5 *Laertes.*   It well appears. But tell me
   Why you proceeded not against these feats
   So crimeful and so capital in nature,
   As by your safety, wisdom, all things else,
   You mainly were stirred up.
   King.   O, for two special reasons,
10 Which may to you perhaps seem much unsinewed,
   But yet to me they're strong. The queen his mother
   Lives almost by his looks, and for myself —

   25 *bore* caliber (as of a gun) IV, vii, 6 *feats* deeds 7 *capital* punishable
by death 9 *mainly* powerfully

My virtue or my plague, be it either which —
She is so conjunctive to my life and soul
That, as the star moves not but in his sphere,   15
I could not but by her. The other motive
Why to a public count I might not go
Is the great love the general gender bear him,
Who, dipping all his faults in their affection,
Would, like the spring that turneth wood to stone,   20
Convert his gyves to graces; so that my arrows,
Too slightly timbered for so loud a wind,
Would have reverted to my bow again,
And not where I had aimed them.

Laertes. And so have I a noble father lost,   25
A sister driven into desp'rate terms,
Whose worth, if praises may go back again,
Stood challenger on mount of all the age
For her perfections. But my revenge will come.

King. Break not your sleeps for that. You must not think   30
That we are made of stuff so flat and dull
That we can let our beard be shook with danger,
And think it pastime. You shortly shall hear more.
I loved your father, and we love ourself,
And that, I hope, will teach you to imagine —   35

Enter a Messenger with letters.

[How now? What news?]
Messenger.   [Letters, my lord, from Hamlet:]
These to your majesty, this to the queen.
King. From Hamlet? Who brought them?
Messenger. Sailors, my lord, they say; I saw them not.

---

14 *conjunctive* closely united   17 *count* trial, accounting   18 *general gender*
common people   21 *gyves* fetters   26 *terms* circumstances   27 *back again*
i.e. to her better circumstances   28 *on mount* on a height

40 They were given me by Claudio; he received them
    Of him that brought them.

King.   Laertes, you shall hear them. —
    Leave us.   *[Exit Messenger.]*
    [Reads] 'High and mighty, you shall know I am set naked
    on your kingdom. To-morrow shall I beg leave to see
45 your kingly eyes; when I shall (first asking your pardon
    thereunto) recount the occasion of my sudden and more
    strange return.   HAMLET.'
    What should this mean? Are all the rest come back?
    Or is it some abuse, and no such thing?

Laertes. Know you the hand?

50 *King.*   'Tis Hamlet's character. 'Naked'!
    And in a postscript here, he says 'alone.'
    Can you devise me?

Laertes. I am lost in it, my lord. But let him come.
    It warms the very sickness in my heart
55 That I shall live and tell him to his teeth,
    'Thus diddest thou.'

King.   If it be so, Laertes
    (As how should it be so? how otherwise?),
    Will you be ruled by me?

Laertes.   Ay, my lord,
    So you will not o'errule me to a peace.

60 *King.* To thine own peace. If he be now returned,
    As checking at his voyage, and that he means
    No more to undertake it, I will work him
    To an exploit now ripe in my device,
    Under the which he shall not choose but fall;
65 And for his death no wind of blame shall breathe,

43 *naked* destitute   49 *abuse* imposture   50 *character* handwriting   52 *devise* explain to   61 *checking at* turning aside from (like a falcon turning from its quarry for other prey)

But even his mother shall uncharge the practice
And call it accident.
Laertes.   My lord, I will be ruled;
The rather if you could devise it so
That I might be the organ.
King.   It falls right.
You have been talked of since your travel much,   70
And that in Hamlet's hearing, for a quality
Wherein they say you shine. Your sum of parts
Did not together pluck such envy from him
As did that one, and that, in my regard,
Of the unworthiest siege.
Laertes.   What part is that, my lord?   75
King. A very riband in the cap of youth,
Yet needful too, for youth no less becomes
The light and careless livery that it wears
Than settled age his sables and his weeds,
Importing health and graveness. Two months since   80
Here was a gentleman of Normandy.
I have seen myself, and served against, the French,
And they can well on horseback, but this gallant
Had witchcraft in't. He grew unto his seat,
And to such wondrous doing brought his horse   85
As had he been incorpsed and demi-natured
With the brave beast. So far he topped my thought
That I, in forgery of shapes and tricks,
Come short of what he did.

---

66 *uncharge the practice* acquit the stratagem of being a plot   69 *organ* instrument   75 *siege* seat, rank   76 *riband* decoration   78 *livery* distinctive attire   79 *sables* dignified robes richly furred with sable   *weeds* distinctive garments   80 *health* welfare, prosperity   83 *can well* can perform well
86 *incorpsed* made one body   *demi-natured* made sharer of nature half and
half (as man shares with horse in the centaur)   87 *topped* excelled   *thought*
imagination of possibilities   88 *forgery* invention

Laertes.   A Norman was't?

90 *King.* A Norman.

Laertes. Upon my life, Lamord.

King.   The very same.

Laertes. I know him well. He is the brooch indeed
    And gem of all the nation.

King. He made confession of you,

95 And gave you such a masterly report
    For art and exercise in your defense,
    And for your rapier most especial,
    That he cried out 'twould be a sight indeed
    If one could match you. The scrimers of their nation

100 He swore had neither motion, guard, nor eye,
    If you opposed them. Sir, this report of his
    Did Hamlet so envenom with his envy
    That he could nothing do but wish and beg
    Your sudden coming o'er to play with you.
    Now, out of this —

105 *Laertes.*   What out of this, my lord?

King. Laertes, was your father dear to you?
    Or are you like the painting of a sorrow,
    A face without a heart?

Laertes.   Why ask you this?

King. Not that I think you did not love your father,

110 But that I know love is begun by time,
    And that I see, in passages of proof,
    Time qualifies the spark and fire of it.
    There lives within the very flame of love
    A kind of wick or snuff that will abate it,

---

92 *brooch* ornament   94 *made confession* admitted the rival accomplish-
ments   99 *scrimers* fencers   111 *passages of proof* incidents of experience
112 *qualifies* weakens   114 *snuff* unconsumed portion of the burned
wick

And nothing is at a like goodness still,   115
For goodness, growing to a plurisy,
Dies in his own too-much. That we would do
We should do when we would, for this 'would' changes,
And hath abatements and delays as many
As there are tongues, are hands, are accidents,   120
And then this 'should' is like a spendthrift sigh,
That hurts by easing. But to the quick o' th' ulcer —
Hamlet comes back; what would you undertake
To show yourself your father's son in deed
More than in words?
Laertes.   To cut his throat i' th' church!   125
King. No place indeed should murther sanctuarize;
Revenge should have no bounds. But, good Laertes,
Will you do this? Keep close within your chamber.
Hamlet returned shall know you are come home.
We'll put on those shall praise your excellence   130
And set a double varnish on the fame
The Frenchman gave you, bring you in fine together
And wager on your heads. He, being remiss,
Most generous, and free from all contriving,
Will not peruse the foils, so that with ease,   135
Or with a little shuffling, you may choose
A sword unbated, and, in a pass of practice,
Requite him for your father.
Laertes.   I will do't,
And for that purpose I'll anoint my sword.
I bought an unction of a mountebank,   140

115 *still* always 116 *plurisy* excess 122 *hurts* i.e. shortens life by drawing blood from the heart (as was believed) *quick* sensitive flesh 126 *sanctuarize* protect from punishment, give sanctuary to 130 *put on* instigate
132 *in fine* finally 133 *remiss* negligent 135 *peruse* scan 137 *unbated* not
blunted *pass of practice* thrust made effective by trickery 140 *unction*
ointment *mountebank* quack-doctor

So mortal that, but dip a knife in it,
Where it draws blood no cataplasm so rare,
Collected from all simples that have virtue
Under the moon, can save the thing from death
145 That is but scratched withal. I'll touch my point
With this contagion, that, if I gall him slightly,
It may be death.

King.   Let's further think of this,
Weigh what convenience both of time and means
May fit us to our shape. If this should fail,
150 And that our drift look through our bad performance,
'Twere better not assayed. Therefore this project
Should have a back or second, that might hold
If this did blast in proof. Soft, let me see.
We'll make a solemn wager on your cunnings —
155 I ha't!
When in your motion you are hot and dry —
As make your bouts more violent to that end —
And that he calls for drink, I'll have preferred him
A chalice for the nonce, whereon but sipping,
160 If he by chance escape your venomed stuck,
Our purpose may hold there. — But stay, what noise?

Enter Queen.

Queen. One woe doth tread upon another's heel,
So fast they follow. Your sister's drowned, Laertes.
Laertes. Drowned! O, where?
165 *Queen.* There is a willow grows askant the brook,
That shows his hoar leaves in the glassy stream.
Therewith fantastic garlands did she make

---

142 *cataplasm* poultice 143 *simples* herbs 145 *withal* with it 146 *gall*
scratch 149 *shape* plan 150 *drift* intention *look* show 153 *blast in proof*
burst during trial (like a faulty cannon) 158 *preferred* offered 159 *nonce*
occasion 160 *stuck* thrust 165 *askant* alongside 166 *hoar* grey

Of crowflowers, nettles, daisies, and long purples,
That liberal shepherds give a grosser name,
But our cold maids do dead men's fingers call them.   170
There on the pendent boughs her crownet weeds
Clamb'ring to hang, an envious sliver broke,
When down her weedy trophies and herself
Fell in the weeping brook. Her clothes spread wide,
And mermaid-like awhile they bore her up,   175
Which time she chanted snatches of old lauds,
As one incapable of her own distress,
Or like a creature native and indued
Unto that element. But long it could not be
Till that her garments, heavy with their drink,   180
Pulled the poor wretch from her melodious lay
To muddy death.
Laertes.   Alas, then she is drowned?
Queen. Drowned, drowned.
Laertes. Too much of water hast thou, poor Ophelia,
And therefore I forbid my tears; but yet   185
It is our trick; nature her custom holds,
Let shame say what it will. When these are gone,
The woman will be out. Adieu, my lord.
I have a speech o' fire, that fain would blaze
But that this folly drowns it.   *Exit.*
King.   Let's follow, Gertrude.   190
How much I had to do to calm his rage!
Now fear I this will give it start again;
Therefore let's follow.   *Exeunt.*

❧

169 *liberal* free-spoken, licentious   171 *crownet* coronet, woven into a
crown   176 *lauds* hymns   177 *incapable of* insensible to   178 *indued* en-
dowed   186 *trick* way (i.e. to shed tears when sorrowful)   188 *woman*
unmanly part of nature

147

Enter two Clowns.

Clown. Is she to be buried in Christian burial when she willfully seeks her own salvation?

Other. I tell thee she is. Therefore make her grave straight.
The crowner hath sate on her, and finds it Christian burial.

5 *Clown.* How can that be, unless she drowned herself in her
own defense?

Other. Why, 'tis found so.

Clown. It must be *se offendendo;* it cannot be else. For here
lies the point: if I drown myself wittingly, it argues an
10 act, and an act hath three branches — it is to act, to do, and
to perform. Argal, she drowned herself wittingly.

Other. Nay, but hear you, Goodman Delver.

Clown. Give me leave. Here lies the water — good. Here
stands the man — good. If the man go to this water and
15 drown himself, it is, will he nill he, he goes, mark you
that. But if the water come to him and drown him, he
drowns not himself. Argal, he that is not guilty of his
own death shortens not his own life.

Other. But is this law?

20 *Clown.* Ay marry, is't — crowner's quest law.

Other. Will you ha' the truth on't? If this had not been a
gentlewoman, she should have been buried out o' Christian burial.

Clown. Why, there thou say'st. And the more pity that
25 great folk should have count'nance in this world to drown

V, i, s.d. *Clowns* rustics 1 *in Christian burial* in consecrated ground with
the prescribed service of the Church (a burial denied to suicides) 3 *straight*
straightway, at once 4 *crowner* coroner 8 *se offendendo* a clownish trans-
formation of *se defendendo,* 'in self-defense' 11 *Argal* for *ergo,* 'therefore'
12 *Delver* Digger 15 *will he nill he* willy-nilly 20 *quest* inquest 24 *thou
say'st* you have it right 25 *count'nance* privilege

or hang themselves more than their even-Christen. Come,
my spade. There is no ancient gentlemen but gard'ners,
ditchers, and grave-makers. They hold up Adam's profession.

Other. Was he a gentleman?   30

Clown. 'A was the first that ever bore arms.

[*Other.* Why, he had none.

Clown. What, art a heathen? How dost thou understand
  the Scripture? The Scripture says Adam digged. Could he
  dig without arms?] I'll put another question to thee. If   35
  thou answerest me not to the purpose, confess thyself –

Other. Go to.

Clown. What is he that builds stronger than either the mason, the shipwright, or the carpenter?

Other. The gallows-maker, for that frame outlives a thou-   40
  sand tenants.

Clown. I like thy wit well, in good faith. The gallows does
  well. But how does it well? It does well to those that do ill.
  Now thou dost ill to say the gallows is built stronger than
  the church. Argal, the gallows may do well to thee. To't   45
  again, come.

Other. Who builds stronger than a mason, a shipwright, or
  a carpenter?

Clown. Ay, tell me that, and unyoke.

Other. Marry, now I can tell.   50

Clown. To't.

Other. Mass, I cannot tell.

Clown. Cudgel thy brains no more about it, for your dull
  ass will not mend his pace with beating. And when you
  are asked this question next, say 'a grave-maker.' The   55

26 *even-Christen* fellow Christian   32 *had none* i.e. had no gentleman's coat
of arms   49 *unyoke* i.e. unharness your powers of thought after a good
day's work   52 *Mass* by the Mass

houses he makes last till doomsday. Go, get thee in, and
fetch me a stoup of liquor.   *[Exit Other Clown.]*

Enter Hamlet and Horatio [as Clown digs and sings].

> In youth when I did love, did love,   (*Song.*)
>   Methought it was very sweet
60   To contract – O – the time for – a – my behove,
>   O, methought there – a – was nothing – a – meet.

Hamlet. Has this fellow no feeling of his business, that 'a
sings at grave-making?

Horatio. Custom hath made it in him a property of easiness.

65 *Hamlet.* 'Tis e'en so. The hand of little employment hath
the daintier sense.

Clown.   But age with his stealing steps   (*Song.*)
>   Hath clawed me in his clutch,
>   And hath shipped me intil the land,
70   As if I had never been such.

                                 [Throws up a skull.]

Hamlet. That skull had a tongue in it, and could sing once.
How the knave jowls it to the ground, as if 'twere Cain's
jawbone, that did the first murther! This might be the
pate of a politician, which this ass now o'erreaches; one
75 that would circumvent God, might it not?

Horatio. It might, my lord.

Hamlet. Or of a courtier, which could say 'Good morrow,
sweet lord! How dost thou, sweet lord?' This might be
my Lord Such-a-one, that praised my Lord Such-a-one's
80 horse when 'a meant to beg it, might it not?

Horatio. Ay, my lord.

57 *stoup* large mug   60 *behove* behoof, benefit   64 *property* peculiarity
easiness easy acceptability   66 *daintier sense* more delicate feeling (because
the hand is less calloused)   69 *intil* into   72 *jowls* hurls   74 *politician*
crafty schemer   *o'erreaches* gets the better of (with a play upon the literal
meaning)

Hamlet. Why, e'en so, and now my Lady Worm's, chapless, and knocked about the mazzard with a sexton's
spade. Here's fine revolution, an we had the trick to see't.
Did these bones cost no more the breeding but to play at 85
loggets with 'em? Mine ache to think on't.

Clown.   A pickaxe and a spade, a spade,   (*Song.*)
            For and a shrouding sheet;
          O, a pit of clay for to be made
            For such a guest is meet.   90

                              [*Throws up another skull.*]

Hamlet. There's another. Why may not that be the skull of
a lawyer? Where be his quiddities now, his quillities, his
cases, his tenures, and his tricks? Why does he suffer this
mad knave now to knock him about the sconce with a
dirty shovel, and will not tell him of his action of 95
battery? Hum! This fellow might be in's time a great
buyer of land, with his statutes, his recognizances, his
fines, his double vouchers, his recoveries. [Is this the fine
of his fines, and the recovery of his recoveries,] to have
his fine pate full of fine dirt? Will his vouchers vouch him 100
no more of his purchases, and double ones too, than the
length and breadth of a pair of indentures? The very conveyances of his lands will scarcely lie in this box, and
must th' inheritor himself have no more, ha?

Horatio. Not a jot more, my lord.   105

Hamlet. Is not parchment made of sheepskins?

82–83 *chapless* lacking the lower chap or jaw 83 *mazzard* head 86 *loggets*
small pieces of wood thrown in a game 88 *For and* and 92 *quiddities* sub-
tleties (from scholastic 'quidditas,' meaning the distinctive nature of anything) *quillities* nice distinctions 93 *tenures* holdings of property 94 *sconce*
head 97 *statutes, recognizances* legal documents or bonds acknowledging
debt 98 *fines, recoveries* modes of converting estate tail into fee simple
vouchers persons vouched or called on to warrant a title *fine* end (intro-
ducing a word play involving four meanings of 'fine') 102 *pair of indentures* deed or legal agreement in duplicate 102–3 *conveyances* deeds

Horatio. Ay, my lord, and of calveskins too.

Hamlet. They are sheep and calves which seek out assurance
in that. I will speak to this fellow. Whose grave's this,
110   sirrah?

Clown. Mine, sir.

   [*Sings*]   O, a pit of clay for to be made
                  For such a guest is meet.

Hamlet. I think it be thine indeed, for thou liest in't.

115 *Clown.* You lie out on't, sir, and therefore 'tis not yours.
For my part, I do not lie in't, yet it is mine.

Hamlet. Thou dost lie in't, to be in't and say it is thine. 'Tis
for the dead, not for the quick; therefore thou liest.

Clown. 'Tis a quick lie, sir; 'twill away again from me to
120   you.

Hamlet. What man dost thou dig it for?

Clown. For no man, sir.

Hamlet. What woman then?

Clown. For none neither.

125 *Hamlet.* Who is to be buried in't?

Clown. One that was a woman, sir; but, rest her soul,
she's dead.

Hamlet. How absolute the knave is! We must speak by the
card, or equivocation will undo us. By the Lord, Horatio,
130   this three years I have taken note of it, the age is grown so
picked that the toe of the peasant comes so near the heel
of the courtier he galls his kibe. — How long hast thou
been a grave-maker?

Clown. Of all the days i' th' year, I came to't that day that
135   our last king Hamlet overcame Fortinbras.

---

118 *quick* living   128 *absolute* positive   128-29 *by the card* by the card on
which the points of the mariner's compass are marked, absolutely to the
point   129 *equivocation* ambiguity   131 *picked* refined, spruce   132 *galls*
chafes   *kibe* chilblain

Hamlet. How long is that since?

Clown. Cannot you tell that? Every fool can tell that. It
was the very day that young Hamlet was born – he that
is mad, and sent into England.

Hamlet. Ay, marry, why was he sent into England?   140

Clown. Why, because 'a was mad. 'A shall recover his wits
there; or, if 'a do not, 'tis no great matter there.

Hamlet. Why?

Clown. 'Twill not be seen in him there. There the men are
as mad as he.   145

Hamlet. How came he mad?

Clown. Very strangely, they say.

Hamlet. How strangely?

Clown. Faith, e'en with losing his wits.

Hamlet. Upon what ground?   150

Clown. Why, here in Denmark. I have been sexton here,
man and boy, thirty years.

Hamlet. How long will a man lie i' th' earth ere he rot?

Clown. Faith, if 'a be not rotten before 'a die (as we have
many pocky corses now-a-days that will scarce hold the   155
laying in), 'a will last you some eight year or nine year.
A tanner will last you nine year.

Hamlet. Why he more than another?

Clown. Why, sir, his hide is so tanned with his trade that 'a
will keep out water a great while, and your water is a sore 160
decayer of your whoreson dead body. Here's a skull
now hath lien you i' th' earth three-and-twenty years.

Hamlet. Whose was it?

Clown. A whoreson mad fellow's it was. Whose do you
think it was?   165

Hamlet. Nay, I know not.

Clown. A pestilence on him for a mad rogue! 'A poured a

155 *pocky* rotten (literally, corrupted by pox, or syphilis)

flagon of Rhenish on my head once. This same skull, sir,
was — sir — Yorick's skull, the king's jester.

170 *Hamlet.* This?

Clown. E'en that.

Hamlet. Let me see. *[Takes the skull.]* Alas, poor Yorick!
I knew him, Horatio, a fellow of infinite jest, of most excellent fancy. He hath borne me on his back a thousand

175 times. And now how abhorred in my imagination it is!
My gorge rises at it. Here hung those lips that I have
kissed I know not how oft. Where be your gibes now?
Your gambols, your songs, your flashes of merriment that
were wont to set the table on a roar? Not one now to

180 mock your own grinning? Quite chapfall'n? Now get
you to my lady's chamber, and tell her, let her paint an
inch thick, to this favor she must come. Make her laugh
at that. Prithee, Horatio, tell me one thing.

Horatio. What's that, my lord?

185 *Hamlet.* Dost thou think Alexander looked o' this fashion
i' th' earth?

Horatio. E'en so.

Hamlet. And smelt so? Pah!   *[Puts down the skull.]*

Horatio. E'en so, my lord.

190 *Hamlet.* To what base uses we may return, Horatio! Why
may not imagination trace the noble dust of Alexander
till 'a find it stopping a bunghole?

Horatio. 'Twere to consider too curiously, to consider so.

Hamlet. No, faith, not a jot, but to follow him thither with

195 modesty enough, and likelihood to lead it; as thus:
Alexander died, Alexander was buried, Alexander re-
turneth to dust; the dust is earth; of earth we make loam;

168 *Rhenish* Rhine wine 180 *chapfall'n* lacking the lower chap, or jaw
(with a play on the sense 'down in the mouth,' 'dejected') 182 *favor*
countenance, aspect 193 *curiously* minutely 195 *modesty* moderation

and why of that loam whereto he was converted might
they not stop a beer barrel?
Imperious Caesar, dead and turned to clay,   200
Might stop a hole to keep the wind away.
O, that that earth which kept the world in awe
Should patch a wall t' expel the winter's flaw!
But soft, but soft awhile! Here comes the king —

*Enter King, Queen, Laertes, and the Corse, [with Lords
attendant and a Doctor of Divinity as Priest].*

The queen, the courtiers. Who is this they follow?   205
And with such maimèd rites? This doth betoken
The corse they follow did with desp'rate hand
Fordo it own life. 'Twas of some estate.
Couch we awhile, and mark.   *[Retires with Horatio.]*
Laertes. What ceremony else?
Hamlet.   That is Laertes,   210
A very noble youth. Mark.
Laertes. What ceremony else?
Doctor. Her obsequies have been as far enlarged
As we have warranty. Her death was doubtful,
And, but that great command o'ersways the order,   215
She should in ground unsanctified have lodged
Till the last trumpet. For charitable prayers,
Shards, flints, and pebbles should be thrown on her.
Yet here she is allowed her virgin crants,
Her maiden strewments, and the bringing home   220
Of bell and burial.
Laertes. Must there no more be done?

200 *Imperious* imperial 203 *flaw* gust of wind 208 *Fordo* destroy *it* its
estate rank 209 *Couch* hide 218 *Shards* broken pieces of pottery 219 *crants*
garland 220 *strewments* strewings of the grave with flowers *bringing
home* laying to rest

Doctor.   No more be done.
     We should profane the service of the dead
     To sing a requiem and such rest to her
     As to peace-parted souls.
225 *Laertes.*   Lay her i' th' earth,
     And from her fair and unpolluted flesh
     May violets spring! I tell thee, churlish priest,
     A minist'ring angel shall my sister be
     When thou liest howling.
     Hamlet.   What, the fair Ophelia?
230 *Queen.* Sweets to the sweet! Farewell.   *[Scatters flowers.]*
     I hoped thou shouldst have been my Hamlet's wife.
     I thought thy bride-bed to have decked, sweet maid,
     And not have strewed thy grave.
     Laertes.   O, treble woe
     Fall ten times treble on that cursèd head
235   Whose wicked deed thy most ingenious sense
     Deprived thee of! Hold off the earth awhile,
     Till I have caught her once more in mine arms.
                         [Leaps in the grave.]
     Now pile your dust upon the quick and dead
     Till of this flat a mountain you have made
240   T' o'ertop old Pelion or the skyish head
     Of blue Olympus.
     Hamlet.   *[coming forward]* What is he whose grief
     Bears such an emphasis? whose phrase of sorrow
     Conjures the wand'ring stars, and makes them stand
     Like wonder-wounded hearers? This is I,
     Hamlet the Dane.   *[Leaps in after Laertes.]*

235 *most ingenious* of quickest apprehension   240 *Pelion* a mountain in
Thessaly, like Olympus and also Ossa (the allusion being to the war in
which the Titans fought the gods and attempted to heap Ossa and Olympus
on Pelion, or Pelion and Ossa on Olympus, in order to scale heaven)
243 *Conjures* charms, puts a spell upon   *wand'ring stars* planets

Laertes.   The devil take thy soul!   245
                                    [*Grapples with him.*]
Hamlet. Thou pray'st not well.
  I prithee take thy fingers from my throat,
  For, though I am not splenitive and rash,
  Yet have I in me something dangerous,
  Which let thy wisdom fear. Hold off thy hand.   250
King. Pluck them asunder.
Queen.   Hamlet, Hamlet!
All. Gentlemen!
Horatio.   Good my lord, be quiet.
            [*Attendants part them, and they come out of the grave.*]
Hamlet. Why, I will fight with him upon this theme
  Until my eyelids will no longer wag.
Queen. O my son, what theme?   255
Hamlet. I loved Ophelia. Forty thousand brothers
  Could not with all their quantity of love
  Make up my sum. What wilt thou do for her?
King. O, he is mad, Laertes.
Queen. For love of God, forbear him.   260
Hamlet. 'Swounds, show me what thou't do.
  Woo't weep? woo't fight? woo't fast? woo't tear thyself?
  Woo't drink up esill? eat a crocodile?
  I'll do't. Dost thou come here to whine?
  To outface me with leaping in her grave?   265
  Be buried quick with her, and so will I.
  And if thou prate of mountains, let them throw
  Millions of acres on us, till our ground,
  Singeing his pate against the burning zone,
  Make Ossa like a wart! Nay, an thou'lt mouth,   270
  I'll rant as well as thou.

248 *splenitive* of fiery temper (the spleen being considered the seat of anger)
262 *Woo't* wilt (thou)   **263** *esill* vinegar   **266** *quick* alive

Queen.   This is mere madness;
And thus a while the fit will work on him.
Anon, as patient as the female dove
When that her golden couplets are disclosed,
His silence will sit drooping.
275 *Hamlet.*   Hear you, sir.
What is the reason that you use me thus?
I loved you ever. But it is no matter.
Let Hercules himself do what he may,
The cat will mew, and dog will have his day.
280 *King.* I pray thee, good Horatio, wait upon him.

Fate will win

                            Exit Hamlet and Horatio.
[*To Laertes*] Strengthen your patience in our last night's
     speech.
We'll put the matter to the present push. —
This grave shall have a living monument.
An hour of quiet shortly shall we see;
285 Till then in patience our proceeding be.   *Exeunt.*

✻

                 Enter Hamlet and Horatio.

Hamlet. So much for this, sir; now shall you see the other.
     You do remember all the circumstance?
Horatio. Remember it, my lord!
Hamlet. Sir, in my heart there was a kind of fighting
5   That would not let me sleep. Methought I lay
     Worse than the mutines in the bilboes. Rashly,

271 *mere* absolute   274 *couplets* pair of fledglings   *disclosed* hatched
281 *in* by calling to mind   282 *present push* immediate trial   V, ii, 6 *mutines* mutineers   *bilboes* fetters

And praised be rashness for it — let us know,
Our indiscretion sometime serves us well
When our deep plots do pall, and that should learn us
There's a divinity that shapes our ends,   10
Rough-hew them how we will —

Horatio.   That is most certain.

Hamlet. Up from my cabin,
My sea-gown scarfed about me, in the dark
Groped I to find out them, had my desire,
Fingered their packet, and in fine withdrew   15
To mine own room again, making so bold,
My fears forgetting manners, to unseal
Their grand commission; where I found, Horatio —
Ah, royal knavery! — an exact command,
Larded with many several sorts of reasons,   20
Importing Denmark's health, and England's too,
With, ho! such bugs and goblins in my life,
That on the supervise, no leisure bated,
No, not to stay the grinding of the axe,
My head should be struck off.

Horatio.   Is't possible?   25

Hamlet. Here's the commission; read it at more leisure.
But wilt thou hear me how I did proceed?

Horatio. I beseech you.

Hamlet. Being thus benetted round with villainies,
Or I could make a prologue to my brains,   30
They had begun the play. I sat me down,
Devised a new commission, wrote it fair.
I once did hold it, as our statists do,

9 *pall* fail 11 *Rough-hew* shape roughly in trial form 15 *Fingered* filched
in fine finally 20 *Larded* enriched 21 *Importing* relating to 22 *bugs* bug-
bears *in my life* to be encountered as dangers if I should be allowed to live
23 *supervise* perusal *bated* deducted, allowed 30 *Or* ere 33 *statists*
statesmen

A baseness to write fair, and labored much
35 How to forget that learning, but, sir, now
It did me yeoman's service. Wilt thou know
Th' effect of what I wrote?

Horatio.   Ay, good my lord.

Hamlet. An earnest conjuration from the king,
As England was his faithful tributary,
40 As love between them like the palm might flourish,
As peace should still her wheaten garland wear
And stand a comma 'tween their amities,
And many such-like as's of great charge,
That on the view and knowing of these contents,
45 Without debatement further, more or less,
He should the bearers put to sudden death,
Not shriving time allowed.

Horatio.   How was this sealed?

Hamlet. Why, even in that was heaven ordinant.
I had my father's signet in my purse,
50 Which was the model of that Danish seal,
Folded the writ up in the form of th' other,
Subscribed it, gave't th' impression, placed it safely,
The changeling never known. Now, the next day
Was our sea-fight, and what to this was sequent
55 Thou know'st already.

Horatio. So Guildenstern and Rosencrantz go to't.

Hamlet. [Why, man, they did make love to this employment.]

34 *fair* with professional clarity (like a clerk or a scrivener, not like a gentleman) 36 *yeoman's service* stout service such as yeomen footsoldiers gave as archers 37 *effect* purport 41 *wheaten garland* adornment of fruitful agriculture 42 *comma* connective (because it indicates continuity of thought in a sentence) 43 *charge* burden (with a double meaning to fit a play that makes 'as's' into 'asses') 47 *shriving time* time for confession and absolution 48 *ordinant* controlling 50 *model* counterpart 52 *impression* i.e. of the signet 54 *sequent* subsequent

They are not near my conscience; their defeat
Does by their own insinuation grow.
'Tis dangerous when the baser nature comes   60
Between the pass and fell incensèd points
Of mighty opposites.

Horatio.   Why, what a king is this!

Hamlet. Does it not, think thee, stand me now upon —
He that hath killed my king, and whored my mother,
Popped in between th' election and my hopes,   65
Thrown out his angle for my proper life,
And with such coz'nage — is't not perfect conscience
[To quit him with this arm? And is't not to be damned
To let this canker of our nature come
In further evil?   70

Horatio. It must be shortly known to him from England
What is the issue of the business there.

Hamlet. It will be short; the interim is mine,
And a man's life's no more than to say 'one.'
But I am very sorry, good Horatio,   75
That to Laertes I forgot myself,
For by the image of my cause I see
The portraiture of his. I'll court his favors.
But sure the bravery of his grief did put me
Into a tow'ring passion.

Horatio.   Peace, who comes here?] 80

Enter [Osric,] a courtier.

Osric. Your lordship is right welcome back to Den-
    mark.

59 *insinuation* intrusion   61 *pass* thrust   *fell* fierce   63 *stand* rest incum-
bent   65 *election* i.e. to the kingship (the Danish kingship being elective)
66 *angle* fishing line   *proper* own   67 *coz'nage* cozenage, trickery   68 *quit*
repay   69 *canker* cancer, ulcer   79 *bravery* ostentatious display

Hamlet. I humbly thank you, sir. *[aside to Horatio]* Dost
know this waterfly?

Horatio. *[aside to Hamlet]* No, my good lord.

85 *Hamlet.* *[aside to Horatio]* Thy state is the more gracious, for
'tis a vice to know him. He hath much land, and fertile.
Let a beast be lord of beasts, and his crib shall stand at the
king's mess. 'Tis a chough, but, as I say, spacious in the
possession of dirt.

90 *Osric.* Sweet lord, if your lordship were at leisure, I should
impart a thing to you from his majesty.

Hamlet. I will receive it, sir, with all diligence of spirit. Put
your bonnet to his right use. 'Tis for the head.

Osric. I thank your lordship, it is very hot.

95 *Hamlet.* No, believe me, 'tis very cold; the wind is north-
erly.

Osric. It is indifferent cold, my lord, indeed.

Hamlet. But yet methinks it is very sultry and hot for my
complexion.

100 *Osric.* Exceedingly, my lord; it is very sultry, as 'twere — I
cannot tell how. But, my lord, his majesty bade me signify
to you that 'a has laid a great wager on your head. Sir,
this is the matter —

Hamlet. I beseech you remember.

[Hamlet moves him to put on his hat.]

105 *Osric.* Nay, good my lord; for mine ease, in good faith. Sir,
here is newly come to court Laertes — believe me, an absolute gentleman, full of most excellent differences, of
very soft society and great showing. Indeed, to speak feel-

88 *mess* table *chough* jackdaw, chatterer 97 *indifferent* somewhat 99 *complexion* temperament 104 *remember* i.e. remember you have done all that
courtesy demands 105 *for mine ease* i.e. I keep my hat off just for comfort
(a conventional polite phrase) 107 *differences* differentiating characteristics,
special qualities 108 *soft society* gentle manners *great showing* noble appearance 108–9 *feelingly* appropriately

ingly of him, he is the card or calendar of gentry; for you
shall find in him the continent of what part a gentleman   110
would see.

Hamlet. Sir, his definement suffers no perdition in you,
though, I know, to divide him inventorially would dozy
th' arithmetic of memory, and yet but yaw neither in respect of his quick sail. But, in the verity of extolment, I   115
take him to be a soul of great article, and his infusion of
such dearth and rareness as, to make true diction of him,
his semblable is his mirror, and who else would trace
him, his umbrage, nothing more.

Osric. Your lordship speaks most infallibly of him.   120

Hamlet. The concernancy, sir? Why do we wrap the
gentleman in our more rawer breath?

Osric. Sir?

Horatio. Is't not possible to understand in another tongue?
You will to't, sir, really.   125

Hamlet. What imports the nomination of this gentleman?

Osric. Of Laertes?

Horatio. *[aside to Hamlet]* His purse is empty already. All's
golden words are spent.

Hamlet. Of him, sir.   130

Osric. I know you are not ignorant —

Hamlet. I would you did, sir; yet, in faith, if you did, it
would not much approve me. Well, sir?

Osric. You are not ignorant of what excellence Laertes is —

109 *card* map *calendar* guide *gentry* gentlemanliness 110 *continent* all-
containing embodiment (with an implication of geographical continent
to go with *card*) 112 *definement* definition *perdition* loss 113 *dozy* dizzy,
stagger 114 *yaw* hold to a course unsteadily like a ship that steers wild
neither for all that 114–15 *in respect of* in comparison with 116 *article*
scope, importance *infusion* essence 117 *dearth* scarcity 118 *semblable*
likeness (i.e. only likeness) *trace* follow 119 *umbrage* shadow 121 *concernancy* relevance 122 *rawer breath* cruder speech 125 *to't* i.e. get to an
understanding 126 *nomination* mention 133 *approve me* be to my credit

135 *Hamlet.* I dare not confess that, lest I should compare with
     him in excellence; but to know a man well were to know
     himself.

     Osric. I mean, sir, for his weapon; but in the imputation
     laid on him by them, in his meed he's unfellowed.

140 *Hamlet.* What's his weapon?

     Osric. Rapier and dagger.

     Hamlet. That's two of his weapons — but well.

     Osric. The king, sir, hath wagered with him six Barbary
     horses, against the which he has impawned, as I take it, six
145 French rapiers and poniards, with their assigns, as girdle,
     hangers, and so. Three of the carriages, in faith, are very
     dear to fancy, very responsive to the hilts, most delicate
     carriages, and of very liberal conceit.

     Hamlet. What call you the carriages?

150 *Horatio.* [*aside to Hamlet*] I knew you must be edified by the
     margent ere you had done.

     Osric. The carriages, sir, are the hangers.

     Hamlet. The phrase would be more germane to the matter
     if we could carry a cannon by our sides. I would it might
155 be hangers till then. But on! Six Barbary horses against
     six French swords, their assigns, and three liberal-con-
     ceited carriages — that's the French bet against the Danish.
     Why is this all impawned, as you call it?

     Osric. The king, sir, hath laid, sir, that in a dozen passes be-
160 tween yourself and him he shall not exceed you three
     hits; he hath laid on twelve for nine, and it would come
     to immediate trial if your lordship would vouchsafe
     the answer.

135 *compare* compete   139 *meed* worth   144 *impawned* staked   145 *assigns*
appurtenances   146 *hangers* straps by which the sword hangs from the belt
147 *dear to fancy* very finely designed   *responsive* corresponding closely
148 *liberal conceit* tasteful design, refined conception   151 *margent* margin
(i.e. explanatory notes there printed)

Hamlet. How if I answer no?

Osric. I mean, my lord, the opposition of your person in 165
trial.

Hamlet. Sir, I will walk here in the hall. If it please his majesty, it is the breathing time of day with me. Let the foils
be brought, the gentleman willing, and the king hold his
purpose, I will win for him an I can; if not, I will gain 170
nothing but my shame and the odd hits.

Osric. Shall I redeliver you e'en so?

Hamlet. To this effect, sir, after what flourish your nature
will.

Osric. I commend my duty to your lordship. 175

Hamlet. Yours, yours. [*Exit Osric.*] He does well to commend it himself; there are no tongues else for's turn.

Horatio. This lapwing runs away with the shell on his head.

Hamlet. 'A did comply, sir, with his dug before 'a sucked it.
Thus has he, and many more of the same bevy that I 180
know the drossy age dotes on, only got the tune of the
time and, out of an habit of encounter, a kind of yeasty collection, which carries them through and through the
most fanned and winnowed opinions; and do but blow
them to their trial, the bubbles are out. 185

Enter a Lord.

Lord. My lord, his majesty commended him to you by
young Osric, who brings back to him that you attend
him in the hall. He sends to know if your pleasure hold to
play with Laertes, or that you will take longer time.

Hamlet. I am constant to my purposes; they follow the 190

168 *breathing time* exercise hour 170 *an* if 178 *lapwing* a bird reputed to
be so precocious as to run as soon as hatched 179 *comply* observe formali-
ties of courtesy *dug* mother's nipple 180 *bevy* company 181 *drossy* friv-
olous 184 *fanned and winnowed* select and refined

king's pleasure. If his fitness speaks, mine is ready; now
or whensoever, provided I be so able as now.

Lord. The king and queen and all are coming down.

Hamlet. In happy time.

195 *Lord.* The queen desires you to use some gentle entertainment to Laertes before you fall to play.

Hamlet. She well instructs me.   *[Exit Lord.]*

Horatio. You will lose this wager, my lord.

Hamlet. I do not think so. Since he went into France I have
200 been in continual practice. I shall win at the odds. But
thou wouldst not think how ill all's here about my
heart. But it is no matter.

Horatio. Nay, good my lord —

Hamlet. It is but foolery, but it is such a kind of gaingiving
205 as would perhaps trouble a woman.

Horatio. If your mind dislike anything, obey it. I will forestall their repair hither and say you are not fit.

Hamlet. Not a whit, we defy augury. There is special providence in the fall of a sparrow. If it be now, 'tis not to
210 come; if it be not to come, it will be now; if it be not now,
yet it will come. The readiness is all. Since no man of
aught he leaves knows, what is't to leave betimes? Let
be.

*A table prepared. [Enter] Trumpets, Drums, and Officers
with cushions; King, Queen, [Osric,] and all the State,
[with] foils, daggers, [and stoups of wine borne in]; and
Laertes.*

King. Come, Hamlet, come, and take this hand from me.
                    [The King puts Laertes' hand into Hamlet's.]

194 *In happy time* I am happy (a polite response)   195–96 *entertainment*
words of reception or greeting   204 *gaingiving* misgiving   211 *all* all that
matters

Hamlet. Give me your pardon, sir. I have done you wrong, 215
    But pardon't, as you are a gentleman.
    This presence knows, and you must needs have heard,
    How I am punished with a sore distraction.
    What I have done
    That might your nature, honor, and exception   220
    Roughly awake, I here proclaim was madness.
    Was't Hamlet wronged Laertes? Never Hamlet.
    If Hamlet from himself be ta'en away,
    And when he's not himself does wrong Laertes,
    Then Hamlet does it not, Hamlet denies it.   225
    Who does it then? His madness. If't be so,
    Hamlet is of the faction that is wronged;
    His madness is poor Hamlet's enemy.
    Sir, in this audience,
    Let my disclaiming from a purposed evil   230
    Free me so far in your most generous thoughts
    That I have shot my arrow o'er the house
    And hurt my brother.

Laertes.   I am satisfied in nature,
    Whose motive in this case should stir me most
    To my revenge. But in my terms of honor   235
    I stand aloof, and will no reconcilement
    Till by some elder masters of known honor
    I have a voice and precedent of peace
    To keep my name ungored. But till that time
    I do receive your offered love like love,   240
    And will not wrong it.

---

217 *presence* assembly   220 *exception* disapproval   227 *faction* body of persons taking a side in a contention   233 *nature* natural feeling as a person   235 *terms of honor* position as a man of honor   238 *voice* authoritative statement   239 *ungored* uninjured

Hamlet.   I embrace it freely,
And will this brother's wager frankly play.
Give us the foils. Come on.

Laertes.   Come, one for me.

Hamlet. I'll be your foil, Laertes. In mine ignorance
245   Your skill shall, like a star i' th' darkest night,
Stick fiery off indeed.

Laertes.   You mock me, sir.

Hamlet. No, by this hand.

King. Give them the foils, young Osric. Cousin Hamlet,
You know the wager?

Hamlet.   Very well, my lord.
250   Your grace has laid the odds o' th' weaker side.

King. I do not fear it, I have seen you both;
But since he is bettered, we have therefore odds.

Laertes. This is too heavy; let me see another.

Hamlet. This likes me well. These foils have all a length?

                                    [Prepare to play.]

255 *Osric.* Ay, my good lord.

King. Set me the stoups of wine upon that table.
If Hamlet give the first or second hit,
Or quit in answer of the third exchange,
Let all the battlements their ordnance fire.
260   The king shall drink to Hamlet's better breath,
And in the cup an union shall he throw
Richer than that which four successive kings
In Denmark's crown have worn. Give me the cups,
And let the kettle to the trumpet speak,
265   The trumpet to the cannoneer without,
The cannons to the heavens, the heaven to earth,

---

244 *foil* setting that displays a jewel advantageously (with a play upon the meaning 'weapon')   246 *Stick fiery off* show in brilliant relief   258 *quit* repay by a hit   261 *union* pearl   264 *kettle* kettledrum

'Now the king drinks to Hamlet.' Come, begin.

                                        Trumpets the while.

And you, the judges, bear a wary eye.

Hamlet. Come on, sir.

Laertes.   Come, my lord.   *[They play.]*

Hamlet.   One.

Laertes.   No.

Hamlet.   Judgment?

Osric. A hit, a very palpable hit.

                          Drum, trumpets, and shot. Flourish; a piece
                                                    goes off.

Laertes.   Well, again.   270

King. Stay, give me drink. Hamlet, this pearl is thine.

Here's to thy health. Give him the cup.

Hamlet. I'll play this bout first; set it by awhile.

Come. *[They play.]* Another hit. What say you?

Laertes. A touch, a touch; I do confess't.   275

King. Our son shall win.

Queen.   He's fat, and scant of breath.

Here, Hamlet, take my napkin, rub thy brows.

The queen carouses to thy fortune, Hamlet.

Hamlet. Good madam!

King.   Gertrude, do not drink.

Queen. I will, my lord; I pray you pardon me.   *[Drinks.]*   280

King. *[aside]* It is the poisoned cup; it is too late.

Hamlet. I dare not drink yet, madam — by and by.

Queen. Come, let me wipe thy face.

Laertes. My lord, I'll hit him now.

King.   I do not think't.

Laertes. *[aside]* And yet it is almost against my conscience.   285

Hamlet. Come for the third, Laertes. You but dally.

276 *fat* not physically fit, out of training   277 *napkin* handkerchief
278 *carouses* drinks a toast

I pray you pass with your best violence;
I am afeard you make a wanton of me.
Laertes. Say you so? Come on.   *[They play.]*
290 *Osric.* Nothing neither way.
Laertes. Have at you now!

> *[In scuffling they change rapiers, and both are wounded*
> *with the poisoned weapon.]*

King.   Part them. They are incensed.
Hamlet. Nay, come — again!   *[The Queen falls.]*
Osric.   Look to the queen there, ho!
Horatio. They bleed on both sides. How is it, my lord?
Osric. How is't, Laertes?
295 *Laertes.* Why, as a woodcock to mine own springe, Osric.
I am justly killed with mine own treachery.
Hamlet. How does the queen?
King.   She sounds to see them bleed.
Queen. No, no, the drink, the drink! O my dear Hamlet!
The drink, the drink! I am poisoned.   *[Dies.]*
300 *Hamlet.* O villainy! Ho! let the door be locked.
Treachery! Seek it out.   *[Laertes falls.]*
Laertes. It is here, Hamlet. Hamlet, thou art slain;
No med'cine in the world can do thee good.
In thee there is not half an hour's life.
305 The treacherous instrument is in thy hand,
Unbated and envenomed. The foul practice
Hath turned itself on me. Lo, here I lie,
Never to rise again. Thy mother's poisoned.
I can no more. The king, the king's to blame.
310 *Hamlet.* The point envenomed too?
Then, venom, to thy work.   *[Hurts the King.]*

---

288 *wanton* pampered child   295 *woodcock* a bird reputed to be stupid and
easily trapped   *springe* trap   297 *sounds* swoons   306 *Unbated* unblunted
practice stratagem

All. Treason! treason!

King. O, yet defend me, friends. I am but hurt.

Hamlet. Here, thou incestuous, murd'rous, damnèd Dane,
   Drink off this potion. Is thy union here?   315
   Follow my mother.   *[King dies.]*

Laertes.   He is justly served.
   It is a poison tempered by himself.
   Exchange forgiveness with me, noble Hamlet.
   Mine and my father's death come not upon thee,
   Nor thine on me!   *[Dies.]* 320

Hamlet. Heaven make thee free of it! I follow thee.
   I am dead, Horatio. Wretched queen, adieu!
   You that look pale and tremble at this chance,
   That are but mutes or audience to this act,
   Had I but time — as this fell sergeant, Death,   325
   Is strict in his arrest — O, I could tell you —
   But let it be. Horatio, I am dead;
   Thou livest; report me and my cause aright
   To the unsatisfied.

Horatio.   Never believe it.
   I am more an antique Roman than a Dane.   330
   Here's yet some liquor left.

Hamlet.   As th' art a man,
   Give me the cup. Let go. By heaven, I'll ha't!
   O God, Horatio, what a wounded name,
   Things standing thus unknown, shall live behind me!
   If thou didst ever hold me in thy heart,   335
   Absent thee from felicity awhile,
   And in this harsh world draw thy breath in pain,
   To tell my story.   *A march afar off.*
              What warlike noise is this?

317 *tempered* mixed   324 *mutes* actors in a play who speak no lines
325 *sergeant* sheriff's officer

      Osric. Young Fortinbras, with conquest come from Poland,
340   To the ambassadors of England gives
      This warlike volley.
      Hamlet.   O, I die, Horatio!
      The potent poison quite o'ercrows my spirit.
      I cannot live to hear the news from England,
      But I do prophesy th' election lights
345   On Fortinbras. He has my dying voice.
      So tell him, with th' occurrents, more and less,
      Which have solicited – the rest is silence.   *Dies.*
      Horatio. Now cracks a noble heart. Good night, sweet
         prince,
      And flights of angels sing thee to thy rest! *[March within.]*
350   Why does the drum come hither?

      Enter Fortinbras, with the Ambassadors [and with his train
         of Drum, Colors, and Attendants].

      Fortinbras. Where is this sight?
      Horatio.   What is it you would see?
      If aught of woe or wonder, cease your search.
      Fortinbras. This quarry cries on havoc. O proud Death,
      What feast is toward in thine eternal cell
355   That thou so many princes at a shot
      So bloodily hast struck?
      Ambassador.   The sight is dismal;
      And our affairs from England come too late.
      The ears are senseless that should give us hearing
      To tell him his commandment is fulfilled,

342 *o'ercrows* triumphs over (like a victor in a cockfight)   344 *election*
i.e. to the throne   345 *voice* vote   346 *occurrents* occurrences   347 *solicited*
incited, provoked   353 *quarry* pile of dead (literally, of dead deer gath-
ered after the hunt)   *cries on* proclaims loudly   *havoc* indiscriminate
killing and destruction such as would follow the order 'havoc,' or 'pillage,'
given to an army   354 *toward* forthcoming

That Rosencrantz and Guildenstern are dead.   360
Where should we have our thanks?

Horatio.   Not from his mouth,
    Had it th' ability of life to thank you.
    He never gave commandment for their death.
    But since, so jump upon this bloody question,
    You from the Polack wars, and you from England,   365
    Are here arrived, give order that these bodies
    High on a stage be placèd to the view,
    And let me speak to th' yet unknowing world
    How these things came about. So shall you hear
    Of carnal, bloody, and unnatural acts,   370
    Of accidental judgments, casual slaughters,
    Of deaths put on by cunning and forced cause,
    And, in this upshot, purposes mistook
    Fall'n on th' inventors' heads. All this can I
    Truly deliver.

Fortinbras.   Let us haste to hear it,   375
    And call the noblest to the audience.
    For me, with sorrow I embrace my fortune.
    I have some rights of memory in this kingdom,
    Which now to claim my vantage doth invite me.

Horatio. Of that I shall have also cause to speak,   380
    And from his mouth whose voice will draw on more.
    But let this same be presently performed,
    Even while men's minds are wild, lest more mischance
    On plots and errors happen.

Fortinbras.   Let four captains
    Bear Hamlet like a soldier to the stage,   385

364 *jump* precisely 367 *stage* platform 371 *judgments* retributions *casual*
not humanly planned (reinforcing *accidental*) 372 *put on* instigated 378 *of
memory* traditional and kept in mind 379 *vantage* advantageous opportunity 381 *more* i.e. more voices, or votes, for the kingship 382 *presently*
immediately 384 *On* on the basis of

For he was likely, had he been put on,
To have proved most royal; and for his passage
The soldiers' music and the rites of war
Speak loudly for him.

390 Take up the bodies. Such a sight as this
Becomes the field, but here shows much amiss.
Go, bid the soldiers shoot.

> *Exeunt [marching; after the which a peal of ordinance*
> *are shot off].*

386 *put on* set to perform in office   387 *passage* death

Supplementary Notes

I, i, 117 AS Something is obviously wrong with the transition of thought. The conjecture that some preceding matter has been left out of the text is perhaps as good as any.

I, ii, 129 SULLIED Use of this emendation of the 'sallied' of the 1604–05 quarto instead of the widely accepted 'solid' of the 1623 folio is strongly recommended by: (1) the implications of the interestingly corrupt 'too much grieu'd and sallied flesh' of the 1603 quarto, into which the intrusive participle 'grieu'd' cannot be thought to have come at the call of an original 'solid' standing in the place of 'sallied'; (2) the example of the 'sallies' in a later passage of the 1604–05 quarto (II, i, 39), which in its context is most certainly to be taken as 'sullies' and which in the folio appears as 'sulleyes.'

I, iv, 37 DOTH...DOUBT This difficult and often altered line is here printed without emendation. In the famous crux of which it is a key part the intent of what Hamlet is saying had perhaps best be taken as a close rewording of what he has just been saying; he may be taken to say that the dram of evil imparts a doubtful quality to all the noble human substance, to his (its) own scandal, i.e. to the detriment of the nobility itself because of 'the general censure' that he has mentioned before in developing at involved length what he offers here with the emphasis of brevity.

III, iv, 162 ALL SENSE DOTH EAT absorbs and lives upon all human sense, not only that made up of the bodily faculties but also the contrasting 'inward' sense made up of the faculties of the mind and soul—all sense, whether low or high and whether bad or good in use (looking forward to completion of the image of custom as a monster of double form, part devil and part angel; see the *Oxford English Dictionary* under 'Sense,' I, 3, 7). The crux of which these words make a part has also produced frequent emendation. See the note following.

III, iv, 163 OF HABITS DEVIL being a devil in, or in respect of, habits (with a play on 'habits,' as meaning both settled practices and garments, which by looking forward to 'actions fair and good' and to 'frock or livery' is subtly involved in the opposition and monstrous combination within the passage of devil and angel, and which contributes to an essential poetic image that tends to be destroyed by a finding of need to emend the phrase, especially when 'devil' is changed to 'evil'; see the *Oxford English Dictionary* under 'Of,' XI, 37, for a showing of the use of the preposition in the sense here given, as in the example, dated 1535, 'he yt is a blabbe of his tonge').

III, iv, 170 AND . . . OUT This line is usually taken to suffer from an omission after 'either' of some such word as 'master,' 'curb,' or 'quell.'

IV, i, 40 AND . . . DONE It would seem that after this fragmentary line there is an omission. Capell's insertion of 'So, haply, slander,' a purely conjectural completion of the line, has often been accepted as providing desired clarification of thought.